222
THE AFTERLIFE

Voices From Beyond

Guy David Uriel

Uriel Publishing Ltd. Liability Co.

222 THE AFTERLIFE

Copyright © 2017 by Guy David Uriel.

All rights reserved. No part of this book may be reproduced or transmitted in any form or by any means without written permission of the author. For information E-Mail
Uriel Publishing Ltd. Liability Co. UrielPublishing@pathian.org

www.urielpublishing.com

Uriel Publishing soft cover edition 2017

Cover Design by Gonen Yacov/GY Creative Studio

Manufactured in the United States of America

Library of Congress Cataloging-in-Publication Data is available from the publisher.

ISBN 978-0-9896697-4-0
ISBN 978-0-9896697-5-0 (eBook)

For everyone

Acknowledgments

It's most important that I thank you, the readers, first. After all, you've taken time out of your busy lives to ask me many questions I never would've thought of myself, and that came through in the essence of this book. You've contributed to the continuation of an awesome and prodigious journey – one predicated upon our thirst for knowledge through questioning. So again, my dearest and deepest thanks.

Ronit Mory, while my spiritual journey may have been solitary at times, your steadfast presence and never-ending barrage of questions have ensured it would never be a lonely one. You remain my friend, my bedrock and my joy. I thank you.

My family at large, here and abroad, you've provided me with the inspiration and support to continue writing. I thank you.

Mark Heidelberger, your exceptional approach and editing abilities have become an integral part of the voices and myself. I thank you.

My special friends, you constantly rain knowledge down on me and, more importantly, instill me with the courage to share your wisdom. As such, this book couldn't exist if it wasn't for you. I thank you.

To the rest, a quote I've adopted: "Grant me absolution from what fault of style and substance critics may find. For them, I and I alone am responsible."

Contents

Introduction		1
Chapter 1	Why?	15
Chapter 2	The Soul	31
Chapter 3	The Passage	47
Chapter 4	Life in the Afterlife	71
Chapter 5	Planes of Awareness	95
Chapter 6	The Power of Change	117
Chapter 7	The Return	133
Chapter 8	Earth / Heaven Connection	157
Chapter 9	God and the Afterlife	189
Chapter 10	The Voices	203
The End and The Continuation		225

222
THE AFTERLIFE

Introduction

And So It Continues...

Ha-ha-ha. Yes, that's me still laughing. And yes, I know it's not the appropriate way of beginning a book – particularly a book such as this – but I can't help it. However, I laugh a bit nervously this time as I realize the magnitude of my path. I'm nervous because what was revealed to me should have been revealed to people of greatness. People we look up to. People like priests, rabbis, holy men, leaders of our communities. Not someone like me. I laugh in an attempt to move through the situation with greater ease and comfort. But wait, why shouldn't it happen to me? In fact, why shouldn't it happen to you? We don't have to be people of enormous importance for good things to happen.

Nevertheless, it happened to me just a few short years ago, and because it did, because it happened to a person whose beliefs are firmly grounded in science, it tested everything I thought I understood about reality. Is this really happening? I had to remind myself that the vast universe is still a mystery and that my belief in God as the almighty creator is still strong, so why not me? Why not allow those (the spirits) who truly follow his way contact a person of their choosing?

Now, if this is the first of my books that you're reading, perhaps it would be the perfect time to tell you that *I speak to spirits*. Spirits who are responsible for the information that's within these pages. Spirits who have yet to divulge their names to me. I highly recommend you read the first book, *111 The Path*, prior to this one, as it lays the foundation for the rest of the revelations in the books to follow. If you did read my first book, then you know that on most occasions I questioned why they couldn't have chosen someone more suitable instead. To begin with, how about someone with better writing skills? Someone with more influence? Someone with charisma? This writing thing does not come easily to me, though I feel I've gotten better at it over time. (I'll let you be the judge of that.) Why couldn't this revelation have come to a person like my copy editor, who has the skills and ability to communicate with you in perfect English? Someone who'll have you scrambling for a dictionary to illuminate the meaning of his *erudite* commentary? (Case in point. Go on, I'll wait.) That's a skill I would love to have been given.

Regardless, I can't shake this obligation; therefore, my journey continues. And so does my silent, stressed-out laugh stemming from the constant disbelief that this is actually happening to *me*. Up until recently, I was only an observer to the many things life has to offer us. By observer, I mean a person who loves to watch documentaries and is constantly searching for knowledge, even if it's only trivial. While such knowledge was at first solely dependent on the efforts of others like archeologists, biologists, astronomers, chemists, physicists, documentarians and the like, now I find myself acting as an active participant in the quest for such knowledge. My role is to tell you how the afterlife works. Me telling you about the afterlife… that *scares me*. I wonder when the laughter will turn into shock.

Many books have been written about the afterlife, so you may be asking, what's going to make this book any different? Well, for one, it's not written using any ancient text. I have not had a "near death experience" nor interviewed anyone who has. My understanding of a different realm through direct spiritual contact allows me to relay information to you. When I accepted the responsibility of acquiring this information by asking the spirits questions about the afterlife, I was reminded that I must first empty my mind from all that I ever knew (or thought I knew) about it. Not an easy task.

At first, I had to ask myself the question, *what do I really know about the afterlife?* Many faiths use the afterlife as a destination for our souls after we die; a necessary transition that every human being on the planet will face sooner or later. The main concept behind this belief is primarily a combination of two things: *body* and *soul*. While the body ceases to function after someone dies, the soul remains alive, continuing toward its ultimate destiny. The afterlife is an important concept in all Abrahamic religions, and followers of each spend countless hours preparing for it. The preparation details may vary, but all of them seem to stress one thing: *that life on earth is a test for eternal life.* In other words, how "well" you do here decides your place over there.

Science has kept a somewhat open mind about the afterlife, although it has failed to provide any solid evidence for or against it, regardless of the myriad researchers trying to prove or disprove that our consciousness continues after death. Similarly, one cannot negate the many claims made by those who have had "near death experiences," a subject hotly debated for its lack of evidence and credibility.

Since my first book was published, I've been repeatedly asked, "Do you really speak to the spirits?" My reply, of course, is always the same. Not to all of them. Just four. But sometimes the inquisition doesn't end there. "Do you *really*?" I'm amazed how firmly people tend to disbelieve such a liberating message while maintaining old, unproven belief systems based on fairytales, superstitions, myths and legends. For those who ask repeatedly, "Do you really?," I answer, "This message is real to me, but if you have a problem with the idea that I receive messages from spiritual beings, then simply regard it as though I'm speaking to my subconscious." As for you, I ask that you not judge me before reading this book. Rather, allow yourself the open-mindedness to glean information from these pages and then judge for yourself. If you want to be critical of others, or in this case me, educate yourself on the subject first so that you have the knowledge and wherewithal to do so.

I realize I've not yet given you the details on how and when this all began, and I think this would be the best place to do it. It all started when I was 25 years old. I would occasionally hear my name whispered softly in my ear, regardless of whether I was alone or with others. I always assumed such sensations were the product of an overactive imagination, and so I chose to ignore them. I remember waking up and turning my head in search of the sound's origin on more than one occasion only to find empty space. Admittedly, I don't recall ever being afraid of the voice, and in retrospect, I'm surprised I never tried interacting with it.

But the real story starts with the numbers "111." I kept seeing these numbers appear over and over for many years before I even started conversing with the spirits, and at first, I was amused by the coincidental nature of it all. I thought how intriguing it was to constantly see "111" in such varied places, from clocks to license plates to my media player, which magically stopped once at one minute and 11 seconds. I must confess it took me a while to understand that this was no coincidence. Perhaps it was my sense of rationality that hindered me from accepting the powers behind the number's meaning.

However, my point of view started changing when the numbers began appearing at greater frequencies. I noticed my attention would be diverted to view the numbers at exactly the right time – often seconds before they would switch to another set of numbers. But the final straw that lead me to search for the meaning of it all was when I came home one day to find several clocks (including the stove clock, which we never even bothered to set) all showing a time of 10:11 when, in fact, it was after 3 pm. The mystery intensified when I realized two battery-powered clocks that were almost always accurate displayed this time, too.

Using logic, I tried to figure out how the clocks could all being showing the same erroneous time, but I kept hitting brick walls with every theory. Battery-powered clocks wouldn't be affected by a power outage, and a stove with a digital face blinks "12:00" after an outage until you change it. Perhaps someone set the time to trick me? Not likely since my schedule at the time was unpredictable and my return home was never the same.

Introduction

Although puzzled by this incident, it soon faded from memory as my wife and son forced me to resume our normal daily routine. The next day when I returned home (at a different time from the previous day), I found myself again staring at the same phenomenon! The night before, I had set all the battery-powered clocks to the proper time, only for them once again to be showing 10:11 upon my arrival! Okay, enough is enough, I thought. This time, *I had to find answers.*

What does it mean? Why the combination of "1-1-1?" When I searched online, I realized this phenomenon was common to many people around the world and that I was not the only one trying to determine the meaning of it. I read many interpretations, and I must say I wasn't satisfied with any of them. For many years, this phenomenon followed me everywhere I went. Over time, it developed into other triple-digit combinations like "222" and "333." It also appeared in more peculiar ways that gradually made me realize this message must be from an unseen power that has the ability to divert our attention in order to show us the numbers. To what purpose I didn't know.

The more I spoke of this phenomenon, the more I realized that even my friends had experienced it. As a matter of fact, my wife who had kept silent about it had experienced it as well. Yes, it was about time for me to figure out the meaning of the messages I had been receiving for so long. Unfortunately, I wasn't sure how to go about doing this. I did, however, feel strongly that before searching for understanding, I had to first accept the fact that someone or something was actually conveying a message to me. Even after accepting this though, how can one find what it is he or she needs to do? Today, I know my destiny, my path. I already understand the meaning of the numbers. I know now that seeing them was my preparation for the spirits to talk to me. It prepared me for the journey ahead.

For a long time, I made no mention of my conversations to anyone other than my wife. I kept it a secret from practically everyone I knew. Why? Mainly because I was afraid of ridicule. I was swayed by the notion that only close family members needed to know about my "dirty laundry." My parents were always concerned about what the neighbors would say. Perhaps it was their way of protecting me from an overly critical and sometimes hostile world. As you probably figured out by now, I no longer fear the critics. I can't say I'm fully immune to them, but if they do affect me at all, it's usually short-lived and quickly forgotten.

So here I am, hearing voices from beyond this dimension, making conversation with spiritual beings, and going through an experience that I don't fully comprehend. This experience should belong to other people, not to me. At least that's what I think to myself. I'm the kind of person who has his feet solidly on the ground. Someone who values scientific proof over untested traditions and blind faith assumptions. One who keeps his mind open, but maintains a healthy skepticism of those who claim they speak with spirits. (I expect no less of you as the reader.)

What do I do? How can I make sense of this experience? I'm face to face with unassailable evidence that life does in fact go on. How do I bring this knowledge out in the open? Everyone I know is going to be surprised, that's for sure. To all of a sudden come out with claims that spirits from another dimension are speaking to me? That's right, me, the guy who would roundly criticize the validity of psychics and mediums?! Talk about a remarkably awkward position to be in! How do I solve this conundrum?

Fortunately, my spirit guides knew this would be a problem for me, and I give them credit for solving it quite elegantly. First, they started by showing me the numbers that aroused my curiosity. This way, by the time they started speaking to me, I was already intrigued. Second, they chose their timing carefully, speaking to me when I was alone or when everyone was asleep to reduce the appearance of me looking foolish or crazy. And third, they didn't mention a word about spreading a message or writing a book until I was both certain of their legitimacy and convinced of my obligations. However, even with all of this mental preparation, I was still hesitant and contemplated many times how to go about actually delivering the message. How do I tell my family and friends of this experience?

Ultimately, I began by telling my wife. About a year had passed from the time they'd first started speaking to me. I chose my words very carefully, fearing she might think me a tad delusional and in need of therapy. In my culture, if you see a psychologist, you're automatically branded a lunatic. Can you imagine what speaking to spirits would sound like? Oi vay! However, to my pleasant surprise, she took it in stride, as if she had been prepped for the occasion (which I later learned was true). She became acutely aware of my obligation to write a book, and she started asking me many questions. It was the beginning of a journey that would change our lives forever.

But now it was time to muster the courage to tell my parents. *That* would take much longer than I expected. No matter how many methods of approach I devised, I still feared their response. I thought of the many times growing up that my mother reassured me she'd love me no matter what, and yet that assurance somehow brought little comfort. I started thinking of the ancient prophets (not that I compare myself to them except by way of analogy) who also experienced these celestial communications, and I wondered if they had an easy time bringing it to light or instead faced the same fears that I do. I would soon learn that I had no choice but to rid myself of this fear.

Before I continue, I'd like to emphasize that seeing the numbers is not the only indication that you're connected to the spiritual world. In fact, not everybody needs the validation of the numbers to know that they share a strong connection with their guardian angels.

As for this book, I must admit it wasn't planned. I know, the title is *222 The Afterlife*, and sounds like an obvious sequel to *111 The Path*, but from where the spirits speak, the numbers act a bit differently and don't necessarily fall in the same order. In fact, I had already invested countless hours writing another book called *333 The Ascended Masters*, which was nearly wrapped up before I stopped to write this one. I know it may not be logical to jump to "333," but as explained to me, the numbers have meanings, and the meanings have a different order and purpose than simple chronology.

So, why am I writing this book that is out of chronological order instead? Because you, the readers, have spoken. I've received so many questions, and the majority of them pertain to the afterlife. From the simplest questions, such as what is it like over there, to complicated ones requiring the use of science and physics just to comprehend the answers. You asked many questions to which I didn't have an answer. Therefore, in contrary to the advice of my spirit guides coupled with your persistence and the desire to satiate my own unquenched curiosity on the subject, I made the inevitable leap to attack this subject first.

I must make it clear that there's been a great deal of development in regard to my communication with the spirits since the time I wrote the first book. Now, not only do I hear them, but I can faintly see them as well through imagery they provide whenever they choose. In fact, if it wasn't for these images, it would have been quite hard for me to describe to you some of their explanations on how the afterlife behaves. For clarification, "they" are four nameless spirits who speak in unison and whose sole message is how to advance oneself *here* so as to advance oneself *there*.

As I receive the words, I'm constantly reminded to never misinterpret their meaning. I'm told to ask for clarification about anything I don't understand. Similarly, if a particular message is not conveyed clearly enough in this book, I ask the same of you – reach out to me for clarity. I've tried to organize the subjects herein as best as I can, but again, I'm no writer. I'm just a messenger. Nevertheless, I've taken great care in trying to explain to you what was explained to me in as easy and efficient a manner as possible. I myself must admit though that while reading back my conversations, even I sometimes find myself scratching my head trying to make sense of it all. That said, bear with me and, as always, you're encouraged to email me with questions.

Just as I started the introduction to my first book with a warning, I would like to issue a warning here as well. Everything you read about the afterlife in these pages is in direct contradiction to what we're lead to believe by the world's major religions. The information the spirits provide is not what's common or guessed at or what's written in ancient texts. It hasn't been conjured by any of the many authors who fail to reveal their sources, nor is it as described by those who've had near death experiences. All I can tell you is what I was told, and no more. If I wasn't told something, I won't make it up just to fill in a gap. I will describe the afterlife in terms that you and I both understand. Moreover, this book is not only meant to describe the afterlife, but to be a tool for spiritual guidance and growth. I know many authors who promise to reveal the "true way" to spiritual enlightenment, but the truth is that there are many ways, and this is only one of them. This is not a book with a bunch of pretty words that don't mean anything. This is the truth as I have comprehended it – the good, the bad, and the ugly. However, I will make you a promise: if you read this book carefully with an open mind, you *will* find your spiritual way.

Why do we even need to know that the afterlife exists? The answer is simple: *fear*. Or more specifically, fear of the unknown. We're afraid that life on this tiny planet has no meaning if it simply ends with the darkness of nonexistence. We want – no, we *need* – assurance that our lives somehow continue. We crave a glimpse of what the afterlife is like. We yearn to *remove the fear*. The spirit guides understand our thirst for answers. After all, we're one and the same. But they've also issued us a warning not to get too fixated on the journey's end, which in this case, of course, is the afterlife. The paths themselves, both here and there, have so much to offer. Since it would take eons for technology to bridge the gap between the dimensions, it's best to concentrate on what's important: *our life here*. Family, friends, work, spirituality. They all contribute to our continued journey through the afterlife.

I might have asked you to have faith that you're about to embark on a great journey, but having faith is in contradiction to the philosophy of The Path and is not what being a Pathian is about. You'll understand soon. I will ask many questions, and in particular the questions you've asked me. I will convey the answers to the best of my ability through my experiences, conversations and the imagery I've received. The believing part of course is up to you (although the spirits don't wish for you to believe per se for reasons that will become clear later on). Just know that the afterlife is not what you're likely accustomed to. It's not some place of serenity in the clouds where the sky is always blue, birds chirp happily, harp music fills the air, and everybody lives in perfect harmony. However, through my conversations, I've learned the afterlife is still a great place that shares many similarities to our dimension and is just as diverse and fluid.

As I'm wrapping up this introduction, there are still so many questions that remain unanswered. However, I pledge to you my sincerest efforts to get as many of those answers as possible within the limits of my conversations and within the size and scope of this book. I'll try to ask questions that encompass a wide range of interests. Of course, it's impossible to put every detail of the spiritual dimension in one book, so expect that these pages will only hold but a fraction of the vast knowledge of the afterlife.

I've been asked many times how my conversations take place, and I will answer that within the chapters of this book as well. Just know for now that the conversations are generally fragmented and vary from subject to subject. I then try to put together all the relevant pieces in a manner that makes sense and entertains.

I would like to thank all of you who have taken the time to send me emails of gratitude and who have shown curiosity. I would also like to thank those who were critical of the first book's message and some of the articles I've written. A few folks have told me bluntly that I've gone astray and that I should contact them so they can show me the light through established religion. In writing back to them, I've told them that, as a Pathian, I'm obligated to keep an open mind to all that's out there, but that I can't solely rely on written words as gospel, including the words I write with the guide of my own spirits. The dialogue usually ends there.

In case you're wondering what it means to be a Pathian, well, it's a word that was given to me from above; a word you won't find yet in any dictionary; a word created to explain a way of thinking that's based on the principles of the Ten Commandments while still breaking from the rigid doctrines of organized religion. To those who don't believe my experiences, I say that's quite reasonable. I'm simply asking that you remain open to walking the path in all areas of your life to see what benefit it brings. And if you still don't believe me, at least credit me with having a vivid imagination. But continue reading nonetheless and see whether a message originating from my "imagination" might still resonate with you. After all, you're here and you're still searching.

So, without further ado, I invite you to join me in my conversations. Just remember, as my guides have said, you personally have the power to decide whether the afterlife is a path or a destination.

Chapter 1

Why?

We're going to have to elaborate more on the afterlife. It seems the first book just increased interest on the subject.

It was inevitable and predictable. Throughout human history, we have wasted precious time searching for the one place we have no need to search for. Instead of concentrating on life, we focus evermore on death. What a waste. We would like to ask why? Why write about the afterlife first, giving in to your curiosity on a subject you have no way of proving? This will only set us back. We must concentrate on advancement in your current world.

You've created this situation.

We did?

Yes. It started on the day you allowed the readers to ask questions. The majority of the questions I receive are related to the afterlife. Readers are craving knowledge, and they ask questions to which I have no answers. Even family members and friends are consistently bombarding me with enigmatic questions about the afterlife. I don't want to be known as that guy who claims access to great knowledge, yet answers "I don't know" to every question. Reminds me of a story, actually.

Ah, the power of a story.

Yes. It's the story of a father walking with his son through the desert. His son asks, "Dad, why is the sun so hot?" The father answers,

"I really don't know, son." "Dad, why is the moon so high in the sky?" "I really don't know." "Dad, why doesn't it rain much in the desert?" "I don't know." Finally, the son stops and thinks. "Dad, does it bother you that I ask lots of questions?" The dad shrugs and answers, "Son, if you don't ask, how will you know?" Of course, this is only a story, but I sound just as silly as the father when I don't have the requisite knowledge. It's like I'm standing in front of this great library with no ability to enter. When I was a kid, I asked my dad many questions, and anytime he didn't know the answer, he would get the encyclopedia and open it to the page where the answer lied. You're capable of providing me with the answers I need. You're my encyclopedia.

What good will this knowledge be to you? After all, there is no way for you to validate the true nature of the afterlife, even if we tell all. Sure, we can explain how the afterlife works, but what good will it be? No one will be able to benefit from this information. If this knowledge was meant for you to know, it would have been apparent to you naturally. Instead, you should direct your curiosity toward matters that happen within the physical world. Within your current state of existence.

We just want to open our minds. Perhaps we need the information in the present so we can relax enough to dwell on the here and now in the future. Now we have an audience. You told me when I was writing the first book that we don't have the power to change anyone, but should someone reach out to us, then we should help them in every way we can. Perhaps this would be a way to help them. Perhaps knowing where we end up provides a needed measure of comfort.

You are correct. Ask your questions. The sooner we get through this subject, the sooner we can continue with our agenda. Just remember, we have seen this before. The more you speak on the afterlife, the more questions on the subject you will receive.

Wait, is that it? No more arguments or objections on why I should avoid the subject? You didn't put up much resistance. I usually don't get much from you in the way of emotions, so it seems odd to me that you'd be accepting this in an almost cheerful and agreeable way.

We are just happy that you continue to write and engage with readers. You have stopped fighting us on the matter of writing. As we mentioned before, you will eventually have no choice but to continue. The persuasion of others will become much more powerful than any of your other personal desires.

I guess I was doomed from the moment I first heard your voices. So, can we get serious now? I'm ready. Are you?

Yes. But in order for us to begin speaking on the afterlife, we would like to ask *you* a few questions first. We would like to know how you expect to benefit from the knowledge we are about to give you.

I'm not sure. I thought you said it wasn't beneficial.

You are asking because you feel there must be some benefit to the living. Think about it and give us an answer at the end of our discussion on the afterlife. Just remember that while we will reveal a great deal, it will represent merely a fraction of a fraction of a glimpse into our world.

What do you mean?

Can you explain life on Earth in one book?

No.

It would require many volumes of books to explain the afterlife just as it takes many books to explain the physical world. Furthermore, not a single fact we will share with you can be substantiated let alone concretely proven.

I think I have an answer already about how at least some of us can benefit from knowing. This answer, however, is grounded in total disagreement with your reluctance to tell us. I believe that knowing where you're going can help a great deal to those who need some guidance on the journey, those who aren't sure where they're going. After all, not everyone is a born Pathian. I think knowing one's path opens up other paths. Even I myself am curious to know where I came from and where I'm going to, and I feel having this knowledge will help me guide others.

That is why you are a natural leader. You will know these answers to be true when you are within our world. But remember, while we may know where we came from, we certainly don't know where we are heading. That is why moments in both the physical and spiritual dimensions are very important, especially those moments that change our course toward an uncharted territory.

You keep calling me a leader even though I blatantly disagree with you. Aren't we not supposed to follow, and therefore we aren't supposed to lead?

You are not a leader in terms of one who commands a physical following, but rather a person whose unique actions and traits persuade others to listen. You are not afraid to question, to disagree when all others agree, to express doubt in the face of certainty. All of these things are what we look for in a leader. How often do you hear a leader asking his followers to question him, doubt him, disagree with him? You are wrong about one thing though.

Which is?

Not everyone being born a Pathian. The fact is *all of us* are born Pathians, but we shall talk about this later.

So, it's all good.

Yes. As for questioning and debating, your readers should do this all the time. Not only with the knowledge that we reveal to you, but rather with all the knowledge that was ever revealed. On the subject of the afterlife, it is necessary that every single person reading this book empty his mind from all that he thinks he knows of the afterlife. It is true that some have gotten a glimpse of the passage to the afterlife, but not a single person has ever made the journey past the border into the afterlife and returned to his body to tell about it.

What do you mean? Wow, I have a feeling I'm going to ask this question many times throughout our conversations.

Take all that was ever written about the afterlife by faiths such as Judaism, Christianity, Catholicism, Islam, Hinduism, Buddhism, Ancient Greek and Egyptian Polytheism, plus personal experiences by individuals, and many other sources telling stories about Heaven, Hell, Limbo, Purgatory, reincarnation, tunnels filled with light and so forth. While we agree that some stories are based on actual principles of the ascension to the afterlife, all of them speak of a spiritual dimension or realm that exists as a sort of intermediary gateway to the actual realm of the afterlife. To top it off, the stories have been taken out of context to fit with an agenda that represents a certain belief. It is something we need to correct.

Correct the stories?

Not necessarily. We are not interested in correcting the factual basis of any story. We are interested in opening minds, freeing them from the constraints of such stories. And if it takes telling a story right, then that is what we must do. But first, we have a dilemma to solve.

Which is?

We are not sure how to go about explaining to you the afterlife.

What do you mean?

Well, first, how do we explain the afterlife when you cannot even conceive your own visible world? Second, how do we explain our world when the senses you currently have limit you in so many ways?

I'm lost.

How do you explain math or physics to an animal?

But we're not animals. We're certainly intelligent enough to understand the principles of math and physics.

What we are saying is how do you explain something to someone who has no concept of that thing, who doesn't even know that thing *exists*? The physical world you live in is a world you know based on your senses – sight, smell, sound, taste and touch. Those senses adept at describing your world are the same ones that cause you to see and feel things that are not as they truly are. These senses exclude many phenomena that occur around you all the time, ones you are completely unaware of. For example, in 2013, a meteor exploded in the sky above Russia. You called it the Chelyabinsk meteor. Other than the obvious explosion and resulting shockwave, there was a second shockwave that most people were unaware of, with the exception of a few scientists. The event created an infrasound wave, well below the receptive capabilities of the human ear, that encircled the globe several times before subsiding. Those waves passed through countless structures and people, but were not felt at all. You can explain hot and cold to the touch of your skin. You can explain the feeling of the wind blowing on your skin and hair. You can describe a sunset and a sunrise. You can even describe radio waves and infrasound waves with the use of scientific instruments. But how do we explain a world that is not felt at all with the senses you possess? Our world is not experienced by touch, taste, smell, sound or even sight. There are many phenomena occurring at this very moment to which even your greatest scientists have yet to be aware, and many more they will never be able to devise a way of observing. So, now can you see our dilemma? How do we explain this in ways you can understand? That is why we never wanted to broach this subject to begin with. Our sole purpose was to remain within the boundaries of your world until the time came to naturally reveal the afterlife to you once again. Unfortunately, that time is already behind us. We have committed ourselves to this book. All we ask is that you open your mind and never dismiss something we tell you as impossible simply because you cannot feel it or imagine it. It can be extremely hard to describe when you have yet to master the ability to control your body's "sense blindness."

What do you mean by "sense blindness?"

Sense blindness is when your senses get accustomed to certain events and eventually work around them as if they were not there. For example, "nose blindness" is a term used to describe how your brain detects and processes scents. When you smell an odor, your scent receptor sends a signal to the brain, which then interprets that signal as that particular odor. Yet after a few breaths, the scent (no matter how strong) will start to fade until you can no longer distinguish it from other scents around you. When you put on perfume and time passes, though the smell is still there, you are unable to detect it. This capability is programmed into the brain as a way to detect new scents that might be dangerous and to distinguish them from ones it has already approved. Human beings and spirits alike are in constant blindness, not only with smell, but with all of our senses. It is therefore hard to describe the many phenomena you are blind to because you were born into this environment. Only through open-mindedness and meditation can you possibly reverse the effect and open your mind and senses to your true surroundings.

You'll have to try your best to explain. I know we're not as sophisticated in our ability to make sense of things as you are, but it can't be that our senses get so much *in the way of understanding the afterlife that we understand* nothing.

Take away your eyes; what do you see? Take away your ears; what do you hear? Take away your nose; what do you smell? Take away your tongue; what do you taste? Take away your sense of touch; what do you feel? Do you see what we are getting at? This is what you know. These are the senses that allow you to interact with your world. We have none of those, yet we are connected to the universe in ways people in the physical world can never comprehend. For you, shutting down all the senses leaves you in total darkness. For us, this total darkness is full of stimuli that we can easily distinguish via senses you cannot even imagine. That is why we cannot explain many things in our world in ways that you can make sense of. And we are well aware that even *we* are limited in some things, albeit limitations we are slowly overcoming, as you will later learn. But don't despair, we will explain plenty. We would like to try the following exercise. Close your eyes and try to imagine the world without your sense of sight. Now, while doing so, imagine a world with no sound. Complete silence. Now, while you are doing that, imagine a world devoid of smell.

That is difficult to do. Even with meditation, my emptiness is not that empty. Moreover, I can't understand how there can be any wisdom or intelligence within nothingness.

Your inability to detach your senses is quite normal, but it underscores the point that while you are in a physical form, it is near impossible for you to understand our world – a world that is full of phenomena bearing no resemblance to the physical universe and one that can only be seen with the senses we possess here. We can argue all day about what is intelligent and what is not, but for that argument, you would need to exercise your imagination to the fullest.

I'll take whatever you can share. I'll use the power of listening. Perhaps it'll be like when we dream. We interact with our dream using no senses – only our mind.

Your mind still uses those senses in making sense of the dreams. When you see images in your dream, it is a mental reference to how you would see them with your physical eyes. Do not despair. You will make sense of our world one day.

I want to make sense of it now, not when I pass. How do you see your world if you have no senses?

We have many senses; just none you are familiar with. We can "see" very clearly and further than any creature you know, but "seeing" would have to be redefined in our terms. We do not use an organ like the eye to see, but as a basis of comparison you can understand, our sense of "sight" would be the equivalent of a thousand eyes multiplied by a thousand more.

Can you explain to me how the afterlife "looks?" For instance, the colors?

You see, this is the problem we have – trying to explain the afterlife through the eyes of a human. The afterlife has no colors or shapes you are familiar with. To understand us as spirits, you must replace your earthly senses and feelings with a multitude of new senses that operate on a molecular level, interacting with subtle variations in light and its inner particles.

Remove feelings, too?

Yes.

But how can the afterlife have no colors? Is the afterlife devoid of colors?

Color derives from the visible spectrum of light in the physical universe interacting with receptors in the eye. Different animals will see colors differently because of this principle, yet the world is still the same. Colors are not the only way to describe the beauty of the world. But we understand you have a problem imagining something you are incapable of experiencing.

I'm starting to understand your dilemma. I don't think anyone is capable of imagining the loss of all senses and feelings, while then connecting to what you describe as a new sense, which I can't even comprehend. I guess we'll have to make do with what you're able to explain.

We shall.

We've already touched on this subject in the first book, but I sense this book would get a bit more attention since more people are interested in the world beyond. So, you say that the physical world advances us to the other. Why is it that most people are obsessed with acquiring knowledge of this process?

The obsession for discovery arises from the fear that life on this planet has no meaning if it simply ends with the darkness of nonexistence. Evidence of the afterlife would mean that fear can be removed; that there is a continued purpose. We have witnessed through our previous contact how an obsession can develop in ways that restricts our whole purpose for living in the physical world. And even though we have warned many not to fixate on an inevitable destiny, but rather concentrate on their earthly path, we get ignored.

But why not think of it? After all, we will end there.

Yes, but it is inevitable no matter what you do. If you only think of saving money for old age, then you will spend your whole life living for *that* moment when you reach old age. But if you place the purpose of your life on the path that takes you toward old age, then you shall live your life experiencing *all* of those moments along that path. A path is much more malleable and fluid than a destination that does not change. Put simply, live in the present, not in the future. With that in mind, what are some of your questions?

Don't you know?

We clarified a long time ago that we are not with you all the time. We do not monitor you 24 hours a day. We do have a life here, after all.

There are many questions that were asked. It's amazing how when I tell people of my experiences with you, they look at me with a combination of astonishment and awkwardness. They're not sure what to make of it. Some withdraw a bit. But in the end, believing or not, curiosity overtakes confusion, and they always find a way to ask more questions. It usually starts with really simple ones and moves to more complicated ones. Like, if there are more people today than before, where are all the souls coming from? Some questions refer to communications I have with you, the authenticity of God, and the validity of the Bible. And, ah-ha, here's a question to get you going that I hear a lot. What is the essence of life? I usually say that I sure hope it's not living in anticipation of the afterlife or of a reward in the afterlife. Every bone in my body tells me those beliefs are wrong.

The essence of life in both dimensions are one and the same. Imagination and creation.

But people want to know that there is a reward for their efforts. That by behaving and acting a certain way, they earn *the right to enter.*

There is no reward.

What is there?

A continuation based on choices you have made.

I'm assuming you'll elaborate further as we speak.

We will.

Shall we begin then?

If we are to begin, we have to get rid of the word "afterlife." It is hard for us, or rather confusing, as the word "afterlife" doesn't really represent where we are. As far as we are concerned, life here *is* the living, while your world is *pre-life*. So, we would like to reinstate the afterlife's most ancient name.

Okay. What would you call this place if it's the place of the living?

We call it "Dorna." It is the word the ancients made up for the place that lied beyond their existence. It is a name we have always preferred.

"Dorna." All right, I'll have to get used to it. For a second there, I thought you were going to say Eden.

Our place is known for many things, including Eden, but Dorna as a name predates Eden by hundreds of thousands of years.

Does Dorna have a meaning?

Yes. "Generation on the move."

Okay, so now that we know we all end up in Dorna, how do we start?

We start at the beginning – the return home. That point you call death and we call the beginning. We start from when you die.

Dying is the beginning?

Not dying, but rather *passing* is the beginning. A little word of advice unlike any you have heard before, which you'll understand later: *treat death as you would birth.*

By celebrating it?

If you truly believe that life continues after your departure from the physical world, then there is no reason for mourning, but rather for celebration of a life of practice and progression. If you know Dorna exists, then you celebrate it because…

You are no longer afraid of dying.

We hope that by the time we finish with this book, your readers will come to realize that though Dorna inevitably lies in their future, the present is extremely important in their current state for the continuation of their advancement.

How about the past? It's a powerful source of knowledge as well. They say to see the future, you must look to the past.

The past is a great tool, yet on most occasions, you let it drag you down. From our perspective, past knowledge serves its purpose only within Dorna. In your world, it becomes an anchor that keeps you from moving forward in your spiritual development. God's law purposely prevents you from remembering past life, and we will teach you that within your world, it requires you to disregard the past and live much more in the present than many of you do.

Now I'm even more confused. I thought I understood from our previous discussions that knowledge has everything to do with our evolution. It kind of reminded me of Buddhism, whose monks preach the importance of living in the present, but nevertheless warn about forgetting the past.

You cannot be so interested in the past and future that you negate the present. To clarify, our evolution and advancement is not dependent on *knowing* a lot, but rather on the act of *acquiring* information. Imagine if there was a way to empty your mind, start fresh, a clean slate. Well, there is. This is the act of true open-mindedness, the act of accruing knowledge that will have a real effect on your evolution in Dorna.

So, a brilliant scientist and a janitor who seek knowledge are the same?

Yes and no.

Huh?

Yes, if they both keep their minds open, allowing an endless flow of ideas. No, if they allow any level of knowledge to hinder their open-mindedness.

Let me see if I understand this correctly. The act of seeking knowledge, of allowing knowledge to flow in, is better for our evolution than a stagnant possession of knowledge.

Yes.

Will this be the first time you've spoken about the afterlife? I mean Dorna?

No, this is not the first time, and it probably won't be the last. We have spoken on this subject to countless souls spanning vast periods of time, in most instances to fulfill the questioner's curiosity. And in most instances, it has backfired on us. Our words have been twisted and misconstrued, while the concept of our need to evolve has been forgotten. Worse yet, additional messages with no basis have been created out of thin air, then mixed with our words to further distance listeners from the truth.

If we are to advance, wouldn't you agree with me that perhaps you should send this message to others who are as receptive as I am at helping expedite your goals?

We always have. We still do. But a fear of sounding insane is holding most people back. Perhaps your writing will help remove that web of fear that they feel.

I feel like a laboratory test subject now. We'll see if it backfires on me. Anyway, I thought the soul was pure and free, devoid of any constraint?

There are limitations in everything. The soul is no different. It is not free from constraint or major limitations.

Wait, I thought our soul was different. That it was not limited.

The soul is a miraculous creation by God who has given souls many tools, just like God Himself has. Not a single tool limits the soul.

Yet you say the soul is not free from constraints and limitations.

Correct.

And so, the major limitation is?

The soul.

Chapter 2

The Soul

The last time we spoke about the soul was when we wrote the first book. Through those conversations, I understood the soul to be the connector between our two worlds, and therefore would be an appropriate subject to tackle before we venture beyond the known world. So, I would like to recap a few already answered questions from the first book, and then continue with a question I previously asked but have yet to receive an answer on. What is the soul? The Hebrew term for soul is "neshama," which actually means "breath." The Pentateuch depicts God blowing the breath of life into Adam's nostrils and then Adam becoming a living thing. Is a soul what's described in the Bible?

We are not sure if it is correct or not, but we can feel a constant connection between us and a divine Creator. We call this connection "neshama." It is an energy that constantly flows through and around us. The further you advance spiritually, the more energy you can observe. And while God's breath is flowing around us in both worlds, it is felt a hundred-fold in spirit form and gets stronger as we advance.

Would you then consider God's breath or something like it to be the connection between us and God?

Yes. From the earliest time that we can remember, we have been connected to God and His creation. Everything that we go through in life helps us refine and perfect our souls. Our journey does not end with death.

Okay. This is where we continue with the unanswered question asked at the end of the first book. I want to know, why are there more souls in the world today than in earlier times? And before you answer this, let me tell you how this question came to be. It seems that this particular question is on the minds of many people and is among the most fundamental in sustaining their belief. According to Judaism, a pure soul is integral to gain entry to the next world, so it inevitably got me wondering how the soul came to be. After all, other than that description in the Bible of God breathing life into Adam, there is not much credible literature speaking to the origin of people's souls. So, where do all the souls come from? Everyone knows there are more people in the world today than there ever was before. At the time of this writing, reliable sources estimate the global population to be somewhere around 7.5 billion. So, if there were only a billion people on the planet at the turn of the 19th century, and just a few thousand during early primitive times, it begs the question, where did all those extra souls come from? This is an argument I hear a lot from people who don't believe we contain a soul, and religions have devised answers I can't accept. For instance, according to the Kabbalah (an ancient Jewish tradition featuring a mystical interpretation of the Bible), the soul that was given to Adam was shattered into infinite fragments following his escapade with God in the Garden, giving each and every one of us just a bit – a small fraction of God's breath – thereby solving the dilemma of how there could be more people today than before. That must settle it, right? Ta-da! An infinite source of soul fragments! But you see, this answer could never satisfy me because even if it's not infinite – let just say it's a lot – then at what point won't we as a population be able to multiply because there's no longer a source of souls? Seven billion? Eight billion? How about 20 billion? What irritates me most is how illogical this is. And unfortunately, there's no recorded answer in the Bible. Perhaps it's time you take charge and lay this enigma to rest.

We told you that for some answers, you must forget all that you think you know. The soul has been a subject of great debate among many who have no substantial evidence to back up their claims, and to be honest, our answer would be no different. We shall explain it, but remember, in the end, keep your mind open and go with what makes sense to you. God's energy flows around us at all times, unseen, though very much felt by us. It is so abundant, it truly becomes a part of us. More accurate would be to say the soul is made through an interaction with Godly building blocks. You must make this distinction because in order to transcend to spirit form, and we shall speak of what that means later on, *you must have a soul*. The soul is the driver behind body and spirit. It can do without a physical body to some extent, but without the spirit, it would not survive…

This doesn't answer my question.

It is probably better for us to be a bit more direct on the subject. What we are about to say will shake the very ground you walk on. We tried to avoid speaking of it at the start, as many would outright reject it, while some might even call it blasphemy.

I'm not sure you can tell me anything more shocking or profound than you already have. I'm speaking to spirits after all.

This is different.

How? Just say it. I'm sure I can handle it.

You are God.

I am?

Yes. Every soul ever created is God. We are all parts of what makes God work.

How did you come to this conclusion?

By the way His energy flows. The way it interacts with us. The way we came to be.

How were you created?

We were created from *nothing*. It is probably better we answer your first question first, which is where did all the spirits come from? For many years, it was assumed that the number of spirits in heaven was fixed, that creation in the afterlife is static, which is completely and utterly wrong. We do not have an end in sight, but we do have a beginning. And it happens daily. It's happening as we speak. It happens from nothing. We understand it sounds outrageous, but the soul is created through God's energy out of absolutely nothing.

How can something come out of nothing? It doesn't make sense. It's exactly the kind of Biblical teaching I've rejected. How God created the vast universe out of nothing and from chaos made order with the ingredients available to Him. Yet you also speak of God creating souls out of nothing.

That is why certain descriptions of the afterlife are better left for the afterlife. However, we have said it now, and we do believe you can make sense of it, even in your world. There is nothing in the natural and immutable laws of God, or physics as might you wish to call them, that contradict the concept of creating something out of nothing.

It's hard to wrap your head around the idea that something can come from nothing.

Not really. Let's use math, the language of your universe. Let's say you have the number seven and we have the number minus seven. Add them together and they annihilate each other, leaving you with nothing. This is just a simple mathematical equation: seven plus minus seven equals zero. Of course, you are aware of this concept. But what if it was reversed? What if you saw it run backwards? Out of nothing, you get seven and minus seven. Real numbers. Physics does not exclude something from running in reverse, and under this example, there is no lawful violation by having nothing become something. Time is another example. Now, we do not say that time is flowing backwards, although we admit neither you nor anyone else has a way of determining that, but under God's laws, we are greatly accepting of the fact that things can "pop" into existence. In this case, we're simply speaking about the soul instead of numbers.

Couldn't it be that we're created from God's energy? That we're a part of God made out of His particles?

No. Our body can only contain God's energy. It doesn't come from it. He created us from nothing. Imagine you hit the palm of your hand with a spoon full of sugar, and from nowhere came a substance that could interact with the sugar particles to contain them. It is the same idea here. His energy interacts with nothing, and in the process, creates us.

Just popping into existence.

Yes. Bursting into existence. However, we would like to qualify something – that this statement may be borne of ignorance. There is a possibility that nothing is not really nothing, but actually something. You see, though our knowledge is plentiful and the level of our understanding is high, our senses still have limitations, as we explained earlier, and even we can be prone to sense blindness. Because we are intelligent, however, we must acknowledge the notion that perhaps we are simply unable to detect or even conceive that what we consider nothing is in fact something.

So, in a nut shell, souls are something that came from nothing and are able to interact with God's particles? But it could just as well be something that came from something? This sounds so confusing. Oddly enough, I do see some logic in it. But more importantly, I admire you for your ability to admit that your understanding is currently limited rather than just making something up that can't be sustained.

It is the power we obtain and sustain as Pathians. It is the reason why you, as early as childhood, questioned the stories of the Bible, the creation of the universe, and the origin of God. Through this commonality, we stand united. United in our understanding.

What is your understanding about God?

That He has no beginning and no end. As creatures of His creation, we will have the ability to observe His energy more and more over time, enabling us to understand Him better. As such, perhaps the confusion of the "nothing versus something" origin argument will be clarified one day, but it will only happen here in Dorna.

Why only there?

Because humanity is in the way. Because just like in the Bible, you have given God human characteristics; yet the God we know is very unhuman. Because only an *unhuman* being can gain the insights and inner workings of another *unhuman* being. However meaningful the descriptions you may give God, your understanding remains far from who God is. You are constantly reminded by many that you should always be in touch with God through your mind and heart. But we all know that the heart as an organ has no bearing on the soul. And the mind limits the soul even though the soul knows no limits when it is within the spirit.

So, are there more souls than living people today?

Abundantly more. But not all souls are in the same stage of development. Not all can control the human body. At least not yet.

If a soul is created out of nothing, then there's no procreation among souls, which means you can't be a creator of a new soul.

We are created from the will of God, and though we ourselves cannot create through the spirit, we can definitely create through the body.

Which means?

We are responsible for our own continuous procreation through the progression of the physical body.

Which means?

In our case, we (the spirits) are the creators and developers of the human body.

Are we really going to head down that path with these claims that you had a direct influence on our evolution, nevertheless our creation? Doesn't God create us?

Incidentally, yes. However, not all of God's creations are *directed* by Him. Most of the time, His creation is a *spark* that causes many movements, and those movements are not directly influenced by Him. It is our belief through observation that God Himself is an observer, a seed planter if you will. He sets winds in motion and watches them from afar as they take shape. Just as you push a loose boulder up a mountain, then let it go and watch it roll downhill, you are not sure which direction it will turn or what damage it will do along the way, or when it finally comes to rest at the bottom, what will grow in its protective shade.

I see. But it's still weird to think that it's within your hand to shape us.

And in return shape ourselves.

Okay, that's even weirder.

Why are you so skeptical of our abilities to shape the human race, not even considering the proven ability of others to shape animals? Have you ever looked at your own creations? How humans have shaped dogs in so many ways and through so many breeds (with great results we might add)? There are more breeds of dog today than there ever were before. There are more dogs today prone to emotional experiences than there ever were before. Just as humans have been responsible for shaping the evolution of dogs, our souls are responsible for shaping the body.

It's so mind-boggling. To think that I as a soul have control and influence on another soul's development, yet I don't even know how I as a soul control my own body. How does the soul control the body?

The same way you control a car.

But we're not cars. You make it seem as though we're just machines.

You are a machine in the sense of a body, but have awareness through the soul. The body without a soul is nothing but flesh and bone. A machine without its operator.

A car without its driver. Okay. But how?

Just as you control a car with your body, and your body with your mind, so is a soul the steering wheel of the body through a web of inter-connecting energy controlling the brain.

Can there be a body without a soul?

No. But there are times when the connection is not perfect. When the body is not within full control of the soul.

What do you mean not always a perfect connection?

Not everything is within our control. The physical body is full of blemishes and imperfections from birth, and even more appear as you age. These imperfections inhibit the soul from fully controlling the body, causing it to struggle at times. Perhaps the use of another vehicle analogy will help explain. Say you have two identical cars, same brand, same model, both with tinted windows that inhibit you from seeing into the car. The only thing that differentiates them is that car B has some engine problems that prohibits it from traveling faster than 40 mph. Now, you put a driver in car A – the one with no problems – and our driver can go as fast as the car will take him. He can cruise at 40 mph or he can speed at 120 mph. Next, the same driver is asked to drive car B. Remember that everything else is the same except for the problems, which are at first unnoticeable. When our driver takes control of this vehicle, he cannot but notice the issue. No matter how skilled he is, he cannot get the vehicle to go faster than 40 mph. To the outside observer, it might seem that one vehicle operator is a bit more careful or even apprehensive. What they do not know is that it is the same driver. This analogy uses a scenario with mechanical problems that are not obvious to the observer, but sometimes the car's issues are a bit more prominent – dents, broken lights, a flat tire, even a missing steering wheel. Imagine how a vehicle without a steering wheel would be perceived by observers! Moreover, imagine the effort it would take for a soul to control such a vehicle!

I think I'm getting the message. So, from that analogy, I deduce that while a body can be handicapped in some way, the soul is fully intact, unable to control the body because of the body's imperfections. Are there souls that are handicapped?

No. There is no such thing. We either exist in perfection or not at all.

I can't imagine what it feels like for a soul not to be in control.

You may find it hard to believe, but sometimes that state is wished for. Sometimes the soul *chooses* that path. Look at it from this perspective: anybody can drive a car that is mechanically sound, but not anybody can drive a car that requires special handling. It is sometimes more satisfying to tame a wild horse than to ride one that has already been tamed. The soul's nature is to tame what is untamable, to challenge imperfection. But imperfections are a rare thing, so the soul is always looking for other ways to challenge itself.

I get all this, I really do. It's just hard to understand from this side why a soul would choose the harder way. If I had a choice between a beat-up sedan and a shiny, new exotic car, I'm definitely going with the latter.

A choice made with tools that blind you from the true purpose of our existence. From here, choices are made with different rationale and objectivity.

You speak of the soul having origins, created out of nothing through interaction with God's energy. Have you witnessed the demise of a soul through natural causes? Or more generally, can a soul be destroyed?

No. Once a spark becomes a conscious soul, as far as we know, it is indestructible. Nothing can hurt it. Nothing can damage its molecular structure.

So, all the bad souls that ever walked the face of the earth are still in existence? Still roaming the universe?

Yes. Even the worst of the worst. But would you believe that the worst of the worst are that way because the best of the best did nothing to stop them? Or help them?

Oh, I absolutely believe that. I don't think anyone in the world would've been able to achieve evilness if it wasn't for good people standing silent.

The soul is quite fragile. It tends to follow easily. It is this trend that is in dire need of change. The soul is like a bucket, designed to be filled and contain knowledge; yet many souls are not aware that this bucket is extremely flexible and can stretch and develop. It is capable of containing much more knowledge than when it was first created. It is this unique feature of the soul that makes us who we are, that makes us tick and wish to grow more.

I always wanted to believe that when we die, when we cross to the other side, all the secrets of the universe are revealed to us in the blink of an eye. That this flow of magical knowledge just becomes a part of us in one instantaneous moment. Wow, what you're telling me – it's as if this knowledge has always been there. Like we always knew it, but chose to forget.

It is kind of like that. Only the secrets of the universe, the secrets of God, are quite different from one soul to another.

How?

The experiences we carry with us while living the way of the Pathian have granted us a better understanding of the universe. It has opened new channels that otherwise would not have been there for us.

Where exactly is my soul right now? Does it exist inside my brain?

Though the soul controls your brain, it resides in another dimension.

Where does the soul reside?

In the passage.

Where is this passage?

It lies between the physical dimension and Dorna. But before we go there, we would like to give you a gift.

The gift of healing others?

You would like that, wouldn't you? But why would we intervene when we use sickness as part of our experiences?

Many people in the world are suffering as we speak.

Most people suffer from illnesses that should not have been there to begin with. And how are they handling it?

Is that really important? Can't you do anything about it?

Would you care for a story?

Yes. Always. Are you going to use a story sourced from a religion?

Yes.

Many have asked me why we keep telling stories that were originally used as lessons on proper behavior within a particular religion. I know you've answered it already, but I think you should clarify it once more. Why tell stories that are intended to convey a religious message?

Because these stories belong to us as much as they belong to anyone else. These stories were written by great souls who came to a realization that set them on a different spiritual path. Such stories can only be understood by souls whose minds are as free as ours. These same stories were often told to religious audiences with little or no effect. They have a strong message that has failed to make a dent in the minds of many religious believers. When we look at a story, we should disregard the frame in which it is placed and instead fixate on the message it contains. We should gauge whether it truly reverberates with us.

I'm ready for your story.

Rabbi Yisroel ben Eliezer, often called Baal Shem Tov, was passing through a town. A doctor who was treating a critically ill patient went to seek the rabbi's help. The rabbi went with the doctor to see the patient, looked at him for a brief moment, then turned to the patient's wife and asked her to prepare some chicken soup for her husband. The husband ate the soup and immediately started to recover. The rabbi remained with the man for another few hours, during which the man's strength returned to him. As the rabbi prepared to leave, the doctor requested a word with him. "This man was about to die, and there was nothing I could do for him! Certainly, chicken soup would not be sufficient to cure him! What did you do?" The rabbi replied, "Illness may appear in the body, but it is caused by the soul. I talked to him as a soul, urged him to turn from selfishness to selflessness. As soon as he agreed, his body responded accordingly." "And the soup?", asked the doctor. "Just soup," replied the rabbi.

Recently, I suffered a toothache so bad, it literally caused me to believe I was about to have a heart attack. The pain was so severe, I felt anxiety run through my whole body. I tried to implement some meditation techniques to steer my mind away from the pain, but I just couldn't. Instead, my mind kept feeding me ideas, which did nothing to help alleviate the symptoms or the anxiety. I rushed myself to the emergency room, and it wasn't until after I had blood tests, an EKG, a chest x-ray, and a CAT scan of my brain that the doctor assured me the problem lied with my tooth. Only then did my pain and anxiety subside. A few mere words of comfort. The problem still remained, yet these words of reassurance took so much weight off my shoulders. And it got me seriously thinking about those who suffer from real illnesses – ones that cause a great deal of pain on a regular basis. How do they fight these illnesses?

Through the mind, the soul has a powerful ability to prolong one's life, regardless of the illness. One has to believe in himself deep down in his soul, and only then can one access helpful energy from the world beyond. However, it is also imperative to gracefully accept one's fate and pass on some valuable lessons to those left behind. In other words, how you exit the physical dimension will have great impact on your continued life as a spirit. Do not forget that the view from our world is dissimilar to yours. We will discuss this plenty at an appropriate time, but for now, the gift we would like to present to you is *a glimpse into our world.*

Isn't that what we're already doing? Isn't that what this book is all about?

We are referring to visual images that will best represent what Dorna is.

The power of healing would've been a nice gift, but I'll settle for the images. A picture is worth a thousand words, as they say.

You obviously have not listened well. The power to heal yourself is already within your ability. It is within the ability of every soul.

According to the Kabbalah, a soul may descend to levels lower than where it lived in a previous life for the sake of correction. This correction is to enable repairs. The Kabbalah states that the soul may find itself reincarnated in the form of an animal, a plant or even a rock. I guess I can understand the idea of animals having a soul, but it's hard for me to fathom under what process a soul will enter a plant, or even worse, a rock. It's further explained that an evil soul who's committed a heinous crime like murder would carry an immense weight, which would force it down into a rock. It all depends on the negativity of its energy. This supposedly is why we hear solid objects move as if they're possessed.

We can live life within an animal, but we do not enter nor *cannot* enter any plant or inorganic matter. Perhaps when we speak of our return to the physical dimension, it would be easier to explain why it would be impossible to reincarnate into a plant, a rock, or any lifeless object for that matter.

And when will I receive those images of Dorna?

You shall receive them when you enter the passage.

Chapter 3

The Passage

You mentioned to me that no one has ever been to the afterlife and returned, yet many have described the afterlife in particular detail after having had a near death experience (or NDE). I consider most of these experiences to be more trustworthy than any religious writings on the subject, especially as they relate to Heaven and Hell.

All are descriptions of the passage to Dorna, not a description of Dorna itself.

Are you certain?

Yes, we are certain. Do you forget who we are and where we are? There are many reasons why we know that no one, whether it be religious figures or those claiming a NDE, have traveled to Dorna, but rather only to the passage – the stage right before the portal to Dorna.

But how do you know they did not?

Besides the idea that we are in Dorna, fully aware of what it is like here, the best clue is that all those who have a NDE speak of a great feeling of love, or of being watched from above by other beings.

And what exactly is it about the feeling of love that precludes the possibility of a living person having seen Dorna?

Love is an *earthly* emotion – an amazing tool we have yet to master. Love can only be felt while you are still connected to your earthly body, or during the process of shedding it while moving through the passage. Once inside Dorna, there are no feelings like love.

No love?

No love.

But…

But what? How can a great feeling such as love be absent in Dorna? For that, you have to be here to understand how unimportant love is to us. As a matter of fact, love is completely useless here.

But how can such a great power – probably one of the most prolific forces shaping us here – be totally absent in your world?

Is it a great power? Do you really believe that? Did you not previously ask us for unique knowledge – a piece of information that would shake the very ground beneath you? There are many things that most of you get wrong, and love is one of them. Love is not a great power at all. It is a power for which you have absolutely no control; one that can bring you up swiftly and tear you back down just as fast.

So, love is not important?

How many times must we say this before you accept it? *Love is of no importance to us.* In fact, it should not be important to you either. We know you will have more questions, but we are equally sure that you will understand this down the road. Just be patient.

What about love for your children? The love that can cause a man to risk his life for the sake of his children's future? How can that not be important?

Many will risk their lives for the sake of their children and the children of others without the need for a feeling such as love. If you care so much about your children's future, respect for their right to explore will benefit them much more than love. Let's not rush here. We will explain it all soon.

The Passage

I'm sure you will. Do you have a name for the passage?

Yes, Tripatoa (tree-pah-toe-ah). It is the bridge to Heavens' gate.

Heavens? As in not one Heaven, but many?

Yes.

Interesting. If no one has ever been to the afterlife, to Dorna, then I can only assume that it's Tripatoa that's been described by those who have had NDE's. But while many elements in their stories seem similar, others are quite different. For example, some would speak of seeing religious figures while others would describe a heavenly landscape while others still would speak of experiencing a darker side. Why is it this way? Why are there so many versions of what I assume is a single passage?

Because, while in the passage, the soul is still connected to the body; as such, the life you lived will lead to a particular experience while you are in there.

So, they are all right?

They are all right. Tripatoa is a way for the soul to morph into its spirit body by shedding all of its emotions and transferring all of its experiences to Dorna, giving each of us a unique transitional encounter. Understand that the transition to Dorna is not a matter of magic or divine intervention, but rather a pure event solidly grounded in the laws of physics, or as we refer to it, the natural and absolute laws of God. Just as the second law of thermodynamics dictates that heat flows naturally from an object at a higher temperature to an object at a lower temperature and never the other way around, so is the behavior of particles that make the soul move back and forth within dimensions acting under slightly different yet generally similar laws. The big difference is that you are unable, nor will you ever be able, to see the particles that the soul is made of while you are in human form.

You speak of a gate to the afterlife – that a passage leads us to the gates of Dorna – but what about the gate to the passage? How does one open that gate?

There is no gate to the passage. In fact, you are connected to the passage at all times. That is why the transition from clinical death to the passage is so easy.

Meaning?

Meaning you are already at the mouth of the passage, only you do not know it. Perhaps it is time to elaborate. The soul must connect between its energy, or more precisely its source in Dorna, and its current position in the physical world. It must do this in order to sustain its energy levels while in a physical form. As we explained in the first book, you sleep in order to allow the soul to recharge itself. When you die, a natural process in the brain foments the disconnection of soul from body, thereby triggering awareness of its location, which is and always was in the passage.

Many "near-deathers" tell of this white light – a tunnel-like feature pulling them upward.

Yes. It is part of the process of leaving the body. It would be easier to explain with the following analogy. Imagine a beautiful sunny day. You are inside a house where all the windows have been shut, where there is not a single beam of light entering the room to indicate that it is sunny outside. No lights. Total darkness. Now imagine all the walls and roof above you are removed in one swift action. You find that you are seeing something completely new, yet you never left your original position. Light fills your eyes, causing a momentarily delay in your ability to see clearly. After your eyes finally adjust, you find yourself viewing a different world than you were in just a few seconds ago. This is what happens to the soul. The instant it finds itself in a new environment, this rapid adjustment to the new setting causes a light-and-tunnel effect. It is not only the environment that causes this, but also a momentary reaction of fear to this new situation, resulting in our vision being constricted to a circular, tunnel-like field.

Is that it?

No. As we have said before, it is a bit more complicated than that. The movement of the soul and disconnection from its earthly senses, emotions and physical limitations mixed with a fear of the unknown generate a whole new range of feelings that can, to some extent, explain what those reporting NDE's have felt.

I read an article about a researcher who speaks of the origin of the white light. He claims that those who looked death in the eyes have usually had an out-of-body experience, seeing themselves floating in the air, looking down on their bodies, and that seeing a white light is a result of the high levels of brain activity that happen moments before death. These brain activities can cause a heightened state of alert that is allegedly the source of the NDE. Through experiments on lab rats, he shows that brain activity spikes right when the heart stops pulsing and lasts about 30 seconds. The section of the brain responsible for sight is so overstimulated as to cause the white light effect. Furthermore, he states that the brain's hyper-connectivity between all of its parts in its final moments gives us the illusion of a passageway, as many near-deathers have described.

Many who do not see the connection between the soul and the brain will always assume the brain is playing tricks on you right before you die. Just answer this. If there is no life after death, to what purpose does the brain intensify its activities right before all the lights go down? How would such brain activities serve our evolution?

Perhaps to ease our way out during our final moments before we pass into nonexistence? If we are to pass into such a state where we are no more, a state of total darkness, why would our brain need to ease our demise? Why not just shut down all at once? Hold on, I'm trying to comprehend a state of nonexistence and non-consciousness, which I must admit is pretty inconceivable. If we are no more, then why would our brain need to ease our pain? Why waste so much energy in its final moments? Why go through this "life review" that near-deathers tell us they experience? Why…?

Unless there is a purpose for it?

A purpose that's required for us to transition to the afterlife?

Exactly. It is an activity we all share – heightened levels of brain activity right before we pass to ensure that all our experiences and memories are moving along with the soul. These memories are an inevitable part of the soul, and it is in this moment when your brain transfers them from physical properties to spiritual properties. Like uploading them to the spirit world.

How can that be? How do you upload your memories from one realm to another? It sounds a bit like fantasy.

Absolutely not. Can information exist in space? You know it does. Information has been streaming from Earth to space in the form of radio waves since the early twentieth century. These electromagnetic waves can be captured by another device. Your brain is such a device, and just like a machine, it is operated through the use of electrical impulses. So, why then would it be impossible for the brain to transmit a signal across the boundary of dimensions? In fact, this transmission of data happens to you all the time within the physical world alone. Did you ever find yourself tuned in to a family member or friend during a discussion, knowing exactly what they were thinking or were about to say?

You speak of mind-reading. Yes, it has happened to me, actually many a time. Sometimes you know what another person is about to say or that person will speak on something you yourself were just thinking about. Is it so? Can we really feel what other people think? Can we actually tune ourselves into their "broadcasting frequency?"

Yes, you can. And you can even improve upon it. But that is for another book. Let us get back to that moment right before we pass. When the brain receives a signal that its source of energy has been extinguished, it has only a few precious moments to upload its significant memories and vast lifetime experiences to the spirit world, which leads to an increase in brain activity. It is the way the brain responds to the soul during its transition. This process actually happens almost every night when you sleep despite your state of health. But in its last moments, the brain has the clearest connections and the upload is done in a more precise way without the chaotic interference of the passage. The data eventually streams right by the soul as it transitions into Dorna, giving it a firsthand look at its memories. Memories from yesterday as well as from long ago as if they were just made moments ago.

Near-deathers always speak of these moments as if they are watching a movie about their lives, reliving it all over again. This is in total opposition to the scientist who claims there can be no consciousness of life without an active brain.

The law of conservation of energy, which nearly every scientist acknowledges, states that energy can neither be created nor destroyed; rather it transforms from one form to another. We know that energy can take many forms and information can exist in many shapes, patterns and dimensions (quantum mechanics). Of course, there will always be those who ignore probabilities, refuse to ask questions, and instead doubt that which has already been proven.

So then, no matter how much scientists examine brain activity in its final moments, they will never have a clear understanding of its true purpose.

Perhaps in a day when technology can help get insight into the afterlife and validate its existence. We know it is possible, but do not recommend it. We do think it is sad though to see that most of the doctors investigating NDE phenomenon conduct their investigation with a predetermined belief that it is all a manifestation of the mind rather than considering other supernatural possibilities, however wild they may be.

What happens to the memories in the event of sudden death like, say, a nuclear bomb that destroys both the body and brain in an instant, thus preventing the brain from uploading the data? Don't laugh at my question now! After all, many people in Nagasaki and Hiroshima were killed in an instant. What happened to their uploading?

No question is laughable. You already know that we encourage all types of questions. It is the purpose of a true Pathian to seek knowledge, and you can only do so by asking questions. As for this particular question, like we mentioned before, you are constantly uploading data on a daily basis while you sleep. It is not as clear as the moment you open the gates, so there is always a possibility that some information will be lost, meaning it is no longer accessible to the soul. But it is very rare and the damage to a soul's development is quite miniscule.

So, this is the reason each of us experiences the passage in a different way? Because the connection we have to experiences from the physical dimension accompanies us as we move upward, uploading as we move through the passage?

Yes. That is why some near-deathers will see holy figures while others will see deceased loved ones from their life. Some of them also claim to see living people passing with them as if they were there in the passage as well. Whatever experiences have left their mark are most likely to be present in the passage.

And how do you explain people who were not faithful to a religion, yet through a NDE claim to have seen a religious figure such as Jesus or the Virgin Mary?

Fear. During their lives, they were always afraid they were wrong. They questioned their state of belief, not sure whether they should follow in the ways of others or not. Over time, this fear built up deep within their subconscious and eventually lead to their most influential experiences.

Fear derived from not believing?

Fear of being *wrong* in their non-belief. This fear is what they see when they are in the passage. The passage has a way of revealing your fears as well as your joys. Fear in life becomes fear in the afterlife while joy in life becomes joy in the afterlife.

There is an old Indian tale that speaks of how, deep inside every one of us, there's a battle between two wolves. The first wolf is evil, angry, jealous, egotistical, full of greed, and lies constantly, while the other wolf is good, joyful, peaceful, honest, full of love and hope. It reveals that the battle is won by whichever wolf you feed the most.

That is true. The passage will reveal to you which wolf you have fed the most.

Many NDE stories are quite positive, but some near-deathers speak of hellish experiences. They tell of darkness, torture, devilish beings and demons. Does that happen?

Yes. Anyone who has had a NDE is unaware of their acquired abilities in soul form and, within the passage, do not realize these abilities have a part in the creation of their new realities. On most occasions, this will translate to divine intervention, and they fail to realize this is of their own doing. Whichever wolf you fed the most becomes dominant in the passage.

But some say they had no reason to experience such an event. That it was in total contrast to who they are.

What you say you are and what your inner conscience says are quite different beasts. We in the physical world are prone to earthly emotions that, in most cases, do not let us see ourselves for who we truly are. You can act bravely, but still be extremely fearful inside. You can show love while secretly hating inside. However, there is no hiding oneself in the passage. Who you are there is who you truly are because the passage is reflecting a manifestation of the soul.

Can we go back to the idea that there are no gates between us and the passage? Could it be that near-deathers who tell of a tunnel with white light speak of the gates between the passage and Dorna? They say the tunnel draws them in, propels them forward at high speed. They claim they are not afraid, but rather peaceful and have no desire to go back.

It is not a tunnel per se, but rather a portal. Not everyone who dies gets to experience the passage in the same way. Some skip what the passage offers altogether and move directly through the portal to Dorna, while others remain in the passage for moments that seem long, although they are in a place that lacks time and space. Near-deathers are more likely to see the passage due to the fact that they are not yet fully disconnected from their bodies. If it was not for that, they would have been propelled forward, falling in to Dorna and preventing them from experiencing the passage in the way they speak of.

I'm not sure I get it. How is it that some see the passage and some don't?

Remember that tunnel vision we spoke of earlier? The longer you stay in the passage, the more you lose that restrictive behavior that limits your sight. Many who have experienced danger in the physical world speak of getting tunnel vision, a phenomenon that allows the brain full power to concentrate on thwarting the imminent danger while simultaneously creating obliviousness to surroundings. As they deal with the danger, they keep on moving, unaware of their surroundings. When danger finally passes, they are in a new location, unaware of where they are or what they have gone through. As for those who experience seeing the passage, it is simple: they stay longer. When the imminent danger is no longer relevant, their vision returns to normal, no longer restricting their ability to see. That is when their life experience is viewed, which shapes their unique journey through the passage. You have to understand that once you are within the passage, you will experience the power of consciousness without the limitation of a physical body and its equally limiting senses. You will be released from the earthly bound of physics in a timeless place of your own making. Can you imagine coming back into your physical body after such an experience? Back into a *limited* body with that memory present for the rest of your life?

They speak of an intense feeling of love and heightened senses while in the passage.

They are still connected to their physical body and thus able to return. As they are traveling (never stationed in the passage), they are followed by their experiences (memories). And since time is no longer an issue, they are able to view all their life experiences in a single shot. Birth, childhood, friendships, love, marriage, parenting, children, grandchildren, the death of loved ones – they all surface as a single image raising multiple, uncontrollable emotions that originate, not from the surroundings itself, but rather from the unaware individual body that is having the NDE.

It makes sense and is in line with what they have described. A life review absorbed in one single moment. I can't imagine what emotions it would raise inside of me if I were to only see the experiences I had in my son's life let alone my entire life all at once. But for what purpose is this "life review?"

This so-called "life review" is a consequence of our transition to Dorna. The memories flowing with us were never meant to be a review of life and do not speak to our fate in Dorna. In fact, it does not serve any purpose in the passage greater than the one it already did in the lifetime of the passer. The experience simply serves us better during our continuation in Dorna, where those experiences are viewed without the filter of human emotions – a trait that is no longer relevant to us.

But this life review does have an effect on the person who returns to his body. It allows him to make some serious life changes.

The passage was intended to be a one-way portal. You are not meant to return unless it was intentionally planned. This experience is only meant to be remembered when you are in Dorna.

Don't you think an experience like this should happen to all of us? The ability to see a life review that enables a person to change? I would expect that viewing your life from a different vantage point can help a whole lot.

Do you really think you are incapable of doing so while you are alive? To view your life from a different vantage point, assess your wrongdoings, and figure out a corrective action? That is why we so often mentioned the power of imagination in the first book and shall speak of it a great deal more soon. That power enables you to do the same thing here. We will not deny the inspiring effect of viewing your memories in a timeless place compared to one where time is constrained; however, understanding your wrongdoings in the physical world has a much greater effect on your position in Dorna than changes made as a result of a NDE. A change resulting from your own discovery rather than the consequence of a supernatural event will have quite different outcomes after you pass.

Anything that requires hard work has a greater effect, I understand that, only I wish it wasn't so. But then, how would one define greatness if everything was easy, right? I was also going to ask you about near-deathers who speak of sensing smells, sounds and taste while in the passage, but I assume it's a consequence of their soul still being connected to their earthly body?

Yes. A manifestation of the soul while it is still connected to the brain.

Near-deathers often live differently after their experiences – more spiritual, down-to-earth lifestyles. They are kinder, less materialistic and more generous. But according to you, it's better for my continuation in Dorna if I live a good spiritual life (as you described in the first book) by coming to these conclusions using my own understanding rather than through a dying experience.

Conclusions through observation have always served us well, but it is not to say that traumatic events do not also serve a purpose. Sometimes, such events are planned beforehand to bring a person closer to the understanding that he must change his ways. And while we appreciate all events and observations that propel our advancement in Dorna, we are discouraged by the side effects a NDE causes.

Like what?

The calamity it brings. Most near-deathers never question the validity of their experience. They are prone to accept life as it is, reducing its challenges to trivial, unimportant clichés. This is a mistake we would like to correct, not only in them, but in those who claim to be Pathians. We shall speak of this soon as well.

You said fear is one of the reasons many see the passage in a dark way. How can we fight this fear? Is it fear of religion being right? Fear we are wrong? Something else?

This fear is rooted so deeply in many of you. It follows from youth and exists as a consequence of your upbringing. It holds you hostage. We must rid ourselves of this fear. We will speak of how to make the right changes at a more appropriate time and will give you the tools to overcome this unreasonable, inherited emotion.

How big is the tunnel? I mean the passage?

It can be tiny or massive depending on your point of view. If we were to compare it to something in your world, then it would be microscopic in size; yet to us, it is quite big. Our world can be big and yet small at the same time.

You mentioned that we fall into it, yet near-deathers describe floating upward at an accelerated pace.

The portal is essentially a tiny wormhole so powerful, it behaves similar to that of a black hole, only again, it is microscopically small and open for just a tiny fraction of a second. As you pass, you fall into this microscopic force where time stretches almost to a standstill. That is why people speak of the passage as a timeless place.

Let me see if I understand you correctly. The passage is also the tunnel to the afterlife so often described by near-deathers and foretold by ancient texts. It's all one and the same.

Yes. It is.

I'm trying to think of a place in the physical world that behaves like the passage.

A market in Old Jerusalem.

Okay. A comparison of the passage to a market in Old Jerusalem should be quite interesting. One particular market there that I truly love is simply a narrow path between old buildings where the ground levels hold many authentic and interesting shops.

The comparison can actually be made with many locations in your world, but we made our choice simply because of your recent trip to Jerusalem. Going down the narrow path at the market from point A to point B at a slow walking pace allows you to see many details. However, zooming down that same narrow path narrows your vision to a fixed point at the end, blurring everything on the sides. You are oblivious to your surroundings. Whether a market or a spiritual portal, what you absorb from it depends on how fast you travel through it.

You say we are all at the passage, even as we speak. At least my soul is there. So, to be able to disconnect completely and move on to Dorna, one must die, right? And if so, is death the trigger that opens the portal?

Yes. The soul is always at the passage. The only way it can ever travel back to Dorna is to disconnect from the body, which opens the portal that allows such travel.

Can the soul resist its natural course and stay in the passage as long as it wants?

Yes. But it is unwise.

There are many stories in the Bible and the Quran of people who enter the afterlife alive, skipping the process of death and disconnection of soul from body. They speak of entering the afterlife with their physical bodies. Some return and some don't. Is that possible?

No, it is not possible. The particles from which we are made would annihilate any physical matter in an instant. There is an order in God's creation. Certain particles should remain in their own dimension as they were intended. If you were even able to enter Dorna with a solid body, it would instantaneously be destroyed with the force of an explosion on a magnitude you cannot imagine. There is only one way to enter Dorna: through a natural pattern of reverse particles. And it is through a similar process that we are able to enter a physical body again.

I know I'm going in circles here, but most of what I know about the passage other than what you've told me comes from near death experiences. One of their defining characteristics, which even scientists have yet to explain, are the stories of near-deathers observing themselves from above, seeing their surroundings, and hearing conversations. How can they see themselves if they are in the passage, or hear if they do not have a physical body at that moment?

They still have a body. They are still connected to all of their earthly senses, only now they have acquired additional abilities that allow them to glimpse into the immediate future – a power we spoke about in the first book.

That's right, glimpsing the future. The 2.5 hours you spoke of?

Yes. Only they are not yet aware of this ability. It gives them an instantaneous view right from the chaotic passage. They can see into their future, and their view is exactly the same as a soul who has just departed. But you do not have to be out of your body to see it. Most of you have the ability to see the immediate future with the use of your connections.

Are we speaking of precognition?

We are. The soul's ability to foresee the future does not diminish in the physical dimension, but rather clouds the limitations of the body, while souls you consider "ghosts" are able to use this ability without being hindered by the physical dimension.

I had a feeling we would start discussing ghosts at some point. It's a common experience I share through you. Seeing them. Only the ones that I see when you open the communications between us are grim, dark, scary, full of pain; they look like they walk toward the light without even knowing why.

Do you want to explain to the readers why and how it is that you can see them?

Sure, let's give them a glimpse into how we do this. Not too much though. I reserved a more detailed explanation later on in another format. But just for now, here's a brief overview of how it works. Ever since I began speaking to my spirit guides, I've witnessed many spirits... Or as we know them, ghosts. It seems that every time a line is opened by my guides, it draws many lost souls wishing to go to where they truly belong. They look gloomy, sad, scary, frightened, and they seem unaware of their purpose, strolling or floating aimlessly without knowing why they're attracted to the light or where they're going. Through my questions, I've learned that our communications open a large enough portal between our world and theirs – one that shines like a beacon of hope, a magnet that draws them from everywhere. They don't even know why they are drawn to it, but nevertheless they come. I must admit I was terrified at the beginning, but just like anything you do repeatedly, I eventually got used to the way they are and no longer fear them. In fact, I've learned that even though they seem scary at times, they're unable to harm us physically. So now, it's your turn to explain what's going on. This is the first time I've shared this with anyone. How did it come to be that they stayed behind? After all, you told me that a portal not dissimilar to a black hole with unparalleled gravity draws us to Dorna when we die.

The passage, just like a black hole, has an event horizon – a point at which you cannot turn back once it has been crossed. So, at any time prior to reaching the event horizon, a soul is powerful enough to drift away. And that happens more than we would like it to. For every time you miss this natural opportunity to go home, you may have to wait ages before you have another opportunity.

How does one "drift away?"

By the power of thought. The power of suggestion.

What is this other opportunity they must wait for once they've drifted away from Dorna? Is it like those occasions when we speak?

Yes. But that is a very uncommon event. When a person dies, a drifting soul can tap into that brief opening generated by another soul and cross as well. It is the reason why many people who are close to death claim they see and feel spirits around them. In the hours just before a person dies, those lost souls who attach themselves to his spirit world connecting line will unintentionally allow him to see spirits around him and even aid in the recovery of his strength for a few hours, bringing clarity to mind.

How can that be? How can you gain clarity if your mind is no longer here?

We have consistently used the terminology of the physical world rather than the spiritual world, but we must make clear that the spiritual world is just as physical as yours in that it is made out of particles and contains mass. It is possible to control a dying body that has lost all of its functionalities via particles, which are unseen by your eyes, but are nevertheless available to the soul.

Some people claim to have the ability to see spirits or ghosts while they are still many years away from dying.

There are some people who are capable of connecting with the passage, or even with Dorna, but lack the ability to make sense of it or the courage to tell of their experiences for fear of ridicule. This connection is misunderstood. A connection that translates to activities like hallucinations, premonitions and other such things is quite real to the person perceiving it, yet it might just as well be a manifestation of the soul in the passage.

Let me see if I understand it right. You're saying that those who see visions of things that are nonexistent in this world may actually see them, but it's really just a symptom of the soul in the passage that we cannot make sense of nor connect to? Would a vision of Jesus or the

Virgin Mary or any other religious figure for that matter fall into this category?

Your beliefs and actions in this world dictate the behavior and actions of the soul in the passage as well as in Dorna. The soul is an imaginary creator. Some are better than others, but all are capable of manufacturing imaginary creations in the passage that may seem real to the observer in the physical world. In the passage, which shares elements with Dorna, the body is stripped of many of its limitations, freeing the soul from its constraints to become what it truly is. You become one with the energy, capable of magnificent creations.

The passage sounds like so much fun, so why is it that all the spirits I see look like they're in such terrible shape?

The passage is just a waystation on our journey. We were never meant to stay there, but to simply pass through. Imagine the passage as if it was a beautiful beach in Hawaii. Picture a view from the movies with no parallel. You are allowed to stay as long as you like and do as you please all the time. But here is the catch: you only have enough money to last for a few days, and you are not allowed to sleep, drink or eat. Now tell me under these conditions how long before this place becomes unbearable? How long before sleep and nutrition deprivation cause you to look at this place in a different way? The passage is only meant as a transition. It is like enjoying the view as you fly over a beautiful ocean, but you would not want to be stuck there. And there is one more important reason why the spirits who reside in the passage seem perplexed and aimless, but let's reserve it for when we speak about dreams.

Are you saying there's a connection between the passage and dreams?

Dreams are made in the passage.

I'll wait patiently for that to be explained. In the meantime, you've put a lot of things in perspective. Now I understand how a NDE can be so misleading. Is this the reason why lost souls look so grim, walking about aimlessly, disconnected from reality?

Yes. The sleep and nutrition deprivation example is an analogy for how they are disconnected from their energy. It is only through the physical body that they can maintain sufficient energy levels. The minute soul and body are separated, they must continue to Dorna or their suffering will increase due to separation from that energy source. They become disoriented and purposeless. It is the same effect a person gets from long stints of not sleeping. It wreaks havoc on the body.

Is that why ghosts look so scary to us?

Let's call them Earthbound spirits.

Earthbound?

Because they are bound to the physical world more so than to Dorna. We told you that the passage and the physical dimension are aligned on the same plane and have more in common with each other than either do with Dorna. In fact, the spirits in at least their first stage of occupancy within the passage, regardless of the fact that they just acquired new abilities, find themselves leaning toward the physical dimension more than the passage itself. They want to be seen and heard. They want to communicate, although the methods in which they were used to communicating are no longer available.

How bad can they become? Were they ever mistaken for fallen angels? Or perhaps for Satan himself?

No, Earthbound spirits are not fallen angels, nor could they be mistaken for them. Their inability to communicate properly negates this possibility. "Fallen angels" is a concept that arises thanks to a different reason altogether. Everyone who follows an ideology has a reason to find evidence that justifies their belief system. If your agenda is to prove demons exist, you will see plenty of evidence that demons exist. If your agenda is to prove the devil exists, you will see evidence that the devil exists. If you believe in the existence of mythical animals, you will see a great deal of evidence for their existence. Everyone engages in this sort of confirmation bias in one way or another. To alleviate confusion, there has never been a figure with abilities like the one you call Satan. Stories such as this originated from those who were able to tune into the passage, which by its very nature can be extremely deceitful. True mediums and psychics who can tune into the passage do not realize how flexible and malleable it is. Each observer sees a completely different passage than others see. This is the nature of the passage. What is true for one observer is not true for another.

So many tall tales and half-truths have arisen because of that.

The passage was never meant to be observed for that particular reason.

Let's get back to the Earthbound spirits. What drives them back to the light? Bear with me. Here's what I mean. If an Earthbound spirit has stayed long enough to lose touch with reality and become a lost soul, dark and purposeless, what drives them to look for that split second of light – the opening of the tunnel by a dying person?

A combination of instinct and a guiding hand from above. Even when madness engulfs us, our souls are begging to be set free. That instinct mixed with the guidance of a powerful source will always be a beacon of hope calling us to come home. We cannot hide from it. Even an Earthbound spirit who remains defiant for a long time will at some point be engulfed with madness strong enough to drive him back in the direction of the light. Back in the direction of home.

It seems NDE's have taken up a large part of this chapter. I have a feeling that this will be the last time I reference near-deathers' experiences or any scientific research on the subject for that matter.

NDE's end before the gates of Dorna. The passage remains the sole source for everything that has ever been written on the subject, including all the great religious holy books.

You have yet to reveal who you are or what your connection is to me. I understand and respect your decision on revealing your identity when the time is right. But if I leave this world before you share it with me, will I know you in Dorna?

The nanosecond you enter Dorna, you will know all there is to know about us and, perhaps more importantly, all there is to know about yourself. We are, after all, a family, although not in the conventional way you are familiar with.

There are many stories told about the entrance to the afterlife. That there is a judge or even God asking questions and that the answers to those questions will determined our fate. I always pondered those questions and tried to come up with different answers than those in the stories. For instance, if asked, "Did you surrender yourself fully to God?", I'm supposed to answer with a resounding, "Yes." But the fact is I didn't, nor do I see any evidence in God's creation requiring me to "surrender" myself fully to him.

We like those stories. In fact, we have a few of them ourselves. There is one we tell that we sometimes, in our darkest moments, wished would have been real. The story tells of a certain soul who arrived at the gates of Dorna. Right after all of his life memories pass by him, he is stopped by God, who then asks him, "Answer these questions properly, and you shall pass to Dorna... I have given you the ability to ask questions. Why have you not asked?" The soul answers, "I am not sure what you mean." "In your lifetime, you have followed a religion without ever asking a single question, even when doubt entered your heart." The soul replied, "I was constantly reassured that this was the way, and when doubt would arise, I did not dare to ask out of fear of retribution." "Are you afraid of people more than me? I am the almighty God. Your fate is and always has been in my hands. Where are those you followed to reassure you now? I am not sure I can allow you to enter. I created you in my image, and I am God. I do not follow. I am a creator, and I gave you this tool as well, but all you did was disbelieve in all that you could see while choosing to believe in what you could not see. It is unfortunate that I must deny you entrance to the afterlife just based on this one question." The soul was terrified by the concept of not entering the only place he had prepared himself for his entire life. "Are you telling me I am not allowed in because I was afraid for my life? Because I did not dare ask questions aloud?" "No," God answered. "The reason you do not enter is that even when doubt came into your mind, you did not dare to ask questions silently within your own heart." Of course, in the end, it is just a story, and we are all granted automatic access to Dorna regardless of our beliefs or the life we lived. But the reality will always remain that the life choices we make in the physical world will have an everlasting effect on our life in Dorna.

Chapter 4

Life in the Afterlife

What do you do in Dorna?

We imagine our way to a better future by swimming in a sea of liquid light.

Huh? A sea of liquid light?

Yes. Our world is quite unique and different from anything you have ever known. It will be a monumental hardship for anyone in your world to truly understand what it is like to experience Dorna firsthand.

Try me.

Well, fortunately, we have access to our memories in the physical dimension, or we would have an even greater dilemma with such description, as we would have no frame of reference for comparison. For instance, what if you had to explain to someone who has never been to the physical world what smell is? You would hit a brick wall, as we can only explain smell through the sensors rooted in our memories. If it was not for the fact that we have these memories, I doubt we would have any ways of explaining it to anyone who has never experienced it for themselves. Can you understand? In simple terms, not having a nose or ever experiencing a smell, nor having the sensory organs or the brain functionality to perceive smell, would render this whole phenomenon useless to us, further inhibiting us from fully understanding it. So, to tell you that we ride upon a liquid sea made out of light, that the particles we are made of can interact and interlock with the particles of a light beam as it is suspended in an almost timeless place, would make no sense to you. And even if you could envision that, it would be a challenge to explain the feelings of connecting and riding said energy beam.

It sounds as though your world is full of amazing colors. I'm trying to imagine this liquid beam acting as a prism would; yet, you said there are no colors in the afterlife, right?

Our world is colorless. At least to us, it is.

Are there no colors, or is it you *who are unable to conceive colors like we do?*

We are aware of how important colors are in your world, particularly when you need them and have the tools to discern them; but considering we remember experiences from both dimensions, we assure you, colors have no importance in our world. If it was possible for our world to be viewed directly from your end, it would fill your eyes with blinding light for the nanosecond before you lost your sight.

But wait, as we discussed before, and as near-deathers keep telling us, the light is not blinding. It's everywhere, yet subtle to the sight.

That is because it is viewed not through your eyes, but via your soul. A soul adjusting between two worlds. The light is energy, and quite powerful we might add. Energy has a way of flowing through us while causing no damage to us in the process. The human body, though great in many ways, is actually quite fragile to intense energy of this sort.

But your world does contain colors, doesn't it? I mean Dorna should be the most beautiful picture of Heaven, where the sky is blue, the fields are green and full of flowers —

These are just descriptions of earthly things. Dorna lacks all of them, yet it is an amazing place nevertheless.

But our legends, our ancient's tales, the holy books —

All speak of earthly images. Once you have concocted a notion of what beauty is, one that is easily fabricated through the misleading images of the passage, it is quite hard for you to imagine Dorna as a beautiful place lacking colors and earthly features. We understand that. We were you once. You have yet to access your memories from here. But to answer your question of what colors Dorna would have if it was possible to view it safely from your end, then to say Dorna is blue is right; to say Dorna is red is also right; to say Dorna is of a color in a spectrum you are completely unfamiliar with would be right as well. Dorna's colors will always look different through whatever mechanism you use to view it.

You mean like colorblindness? Or how animals see the world in a different spectrum? I actually understand this concept quite well. Per your teachings, I'm obligated to remain open-minded, and just because it's hard for me to imagine doesn't mean what you say isn't right. It's simply that by my earthly limitations I'm unable to comprehend some elements – well, actually most elements – of the afterlife. It's just like religions that argue their case from a particular point of view while steadfastly refusing to acknowledge other religious views or even secular arguments, though it's obvious they understand there are different ways to view different facts.

We also share your frustrations on the subject. We shall touch on this in further detail when we speak about the planes of Dorna and how religious beliefs, though dimensions away, still beat loudly here.

You speak of living in liquid made of light. Where does this light come from?

From many dimensions, including the one you are in right now. It is the same light that emanates from the sun and travels from stars lights years away. Light emitted from supernovas, both recent and ancient, also pass through our world. In Dorna, light slows down, and as it interacts with timeless space, the particles that are able to penetrate behave as liquid. We exist at a subatomic level between atoms. A world between a world that allows us the unique ability to interact with this energy and become one.

And you ride those particles?

We ride the light waves just as you swim in water. With minor differences, of course. Without getting into too many details, here is a quick explanation. Our world is like an ocean with many currents running through it, similar in some ways to the Atlantic Ocean and the various currents (such as the Gulf Stream) that run through it. When you swim into the current, the particles of water start pushing your body, carrying you in the direction it is traveling until you either reach the end or manage to free yourself from the current. With this rough description, try now to imagine Dorna as a three-dimensional space where liquid energy is the medium. In this medium, streams and rivers are flowing in all directions. Up, down, sideways, cutting through one another without ever disturbing the others. For us to traverse this three-dimensional sea of light, all we have to do is tune in and out of the particular light currents.

How?

By *becoming* the light. We are able to manipulate the density and vibrations of the particles from which we are made. Imagine us, the spirits, as a fishnet.

Okay, a fishnet. Nice description for a spirit.

When spread, a fishnet allows the water current to flow right through it. But if folded, it becomes less porous and is easily carried by the current. We control our nets to go up, down and sideways at speeds that would be inconceivable to you.

Must feel good to fly. Or swim.

It is better than swimming, better than flying.

Still, it sounds a bit odd.

What is odd?

Well, as an open-minded individual, I won't dismiss it as a possibility, but it's certainly at odds with everything that I currently know.

What do you know that does not comport with our descriptions?

Particles behaving the way you describe. Being porous and then not.

It should not be that odd to you. Your ability to interact with the world is due to atomic bonding, the immense force that holds your body together. If it was not for that, you would fall right through the earth between other atoms. The bonding of your atoms is what allows you to move. It is what allows you to make your way through the world. It is what allows you to exist. Now that is an even more magnificent phenomenon. Do you know the amount of energy required to separate those atoms?

I do. A devastating amount of force.

We can manipulate the distance between our atoms. This ability allows us to be more or less porous as we interact with our environment. The greater the distance between our particles, the more energy we have.

How is it that you can view our world while we can't view yours?

Perhaps an analogy would help explain it. Imagine that your world, the one we call the physical world (and we shall argue about the physicality of it one day) was contained within a computer. Your world is confined to an electronic circuit board and hard drive – an amazing environment made possible by a program and controlled by rules made by a programmer. But you are oblivious to the idea that this world is confined to the parts that make up the computer. We are on the other end, confined to a different set of circuit boards and hard drives that answer to a different set of rules, but are nevertheless connected to your world through a screen that acts in many ways like a one-way mirror, allowing us to view elements of your world. The keyboard is our way of communicating and interacting with you. You, on the other hand, are confined to your world, with no screen or keyboard to communicate with us unless we initiate it first. You will find that no matter how much you traverse the program that operates within the bounds of your hard drive and circuit board, you will never be able to see into ours.

There is an argument among scientists about whether we are living in a virtual reality on someone's computer. Could it truly be that, to take your analogy one step further, we are all actually confined within a giant supercomputer, unable to differentiate the true nature of it all?

It is a possibility.

It is? I wasn't expecting that. I was expecting some profound edict that would give my life purpose. Something other than the theory that I may be operating as a self-aware program in a virtual reality machine. I was expecting you to tell me such an idea was all nonsense.

Honestly, we do not believe we exist in a virtual reality. Throughout the many eons of our existence, we can find no reason for a virtual reality machine that contains worlds within worlds with vast levels and planes. Though we ourselves are creators, we are also participators as well. Why would anyone create a world he does not take part in?

Well, if God did create the world, and per our past conversations, we agree that He does not interfere in our affairs, then what you say is a bit of a contradiction.

We have said God is a creator who does not interfere in our affairs, yet He nevertheless takes part in our existence. To the point of your original idea, the reason we cannot say for certain that we are not in a virtual machine is simple: we are Pathians. Even if our views and experiences tell us differently, so long as this observation exists and its argument is valid, we are obliged to entertain rather than deny it. Besides, even if this theory turned out to be true, life would still be worth it – every last bit.

Sometimes I forget that what I ask others to accept I must first accept myself. It's funny though that you used an analogy to explain why we can't observe Dorna by comparing it to a virtual reality within a computer. But the analogy still doesn't explain the reason why *we cannot see your world.*

The reason we can see your world while you cannot see ours is because our dimension acts more like a receiver, like a black hole that sucks in material and information, while the physical dimension acts more like a reflector. In more scientific terms, as light beams bounce from your dimension into ours, they carry a unique pattern of energy that we can translate into interpretable images and sound, which we have familiarized ourselves with through the many lives we have lived. It is as though we are watching a computer screen. In essence, the light carries information from your planet and other places throughout the vast universe. Our world, though parallel to yours, exists at subatomic levels and behaves in a way that would confound your greatest physicists. Dorna captures those light waves, and what looks to you like an instant passing looks to us like a lifetime. In the simplest words, the physical dimension is a mere projector while Dorna is a vast computer database. It is the reason why glimpsing the afterlife is so hard from your side.

I want to talk more about this, but let's first go back to the part where you said you're imagining your way to a better future. What do you mean by that? I assume that if you chose to initially describe your world using the concept of imagination, there must be a reason.

Imagination and curiosity is and has always been the main driving force that propels us forward. Through our observation and experiences, we realized it is the most important tool we have, one that will better prepare us to help you advance in your world so that we can ultimately advance here. As we said before, by advancing in your world, we can better our position and energy in Dorna. But the tools we have here can prepare us for the journey, for the path in your world.

This is so confusing. Doing something here so you can get better there. Doing something there to advance here to advance you there—

Why is it so confusing? If you need help understanding, imagine a mountain—

Here we go again with the mountains. (Side note: for those of you who have not yet read my previous book, "111 The Path," the spirits use mountains as a metaphor excessively in order to explain The Path.)

The mountains will remain the best analogy we have to explain many things. Imagine an inexperienced person climbing a soaring mountain for the first time in his life. As the novice climber ascends the mountain, reaching about one-seventh of the way, his muscles and breathing begin to betray him. In life, we find that there are two types of inexperienced climbers. The first will call it off and say this is all he can do. He will climb back down, never attempting the endeavor again. The other type of climber will not allow his inexperience to become an obstacle, and will therefore decide he must *become* experienced. The climber who calls it off will always be known as the one who only went one-seventh of the way up, never curious enough to try for more, while the other climber will become a man of experience, descending back down again to regain his energy and investigate new strategies for his next climb. He will exercise and educate himself before climbing back to the one-seventh spot many times just so he can practice, and once he is ready to ascend higher, he will try again; only this time, he will go much further. Every time he climbs, he will reach new heights. Two-sevenths, three-sevenths, four-sevenths, and so forth. Every time, he must come down to train harder, garner more knowledge, learn from his past experiences, toughen up – anything and everything at his disposal to help him move forward. While he is up on that mountain, he will gain new insights regarding what is needed to go higher, which he can use during his preparation at the bottom. These are things he would not have known unless he kept on moving up. Dorna is the mountain, and the physical dimension is the valley below.

You gain insight into Dorna through the physical world, which is your practice ground.

For some of us. There are those who will forever remain on the first level, never practicing going beyond. Allowing fear, weakness and a lack of curiosity to hold them in place.

Your metaphors always have meanings, so I'm assuming that the one-seventh scale you used is important in Dorna?

It is a measurement of a present importance, yes. Emphasis on the *present*. We hope that one day, however, the one-seventh measurement will become a symbol of the past.

Where is Dorna?

It is all around you. It is within arm's reach, however unreachable. We are in a universe perpendicular to yours. You cannot see us, but we can see you. It is a universe that interacts with yours through the particles of the soul.

I'm not sure I can explain it, but I believe I've seen images in my dream of the afterlife. Rather complex images.

Images that are fitted to your understanding.

Are you responsible for that?

We are partly responsible for it. These images were given at a time when you were more susceptible to receiving such information, and during a period when we could send messages with greater ease. We do it when you are sleeping. That is why we ask that you never disregard your dreams, in particular those that you remember. It is quite an effort for us to imprint an image, nevertheless onto the soul and brain for you to remember.

You said I'll get the images when I'm in the passage.

When you are asleep, you are in the passage.

I am?

Your soul is. Dreams occur when your consciousness is in the passage.

Do dreams have meaning?

Dreams do have meaning – personal meanings with personal interpretations. In your case, the images were intended to provide you with a glimpse of our world. As such, we used images that would make sense to you.

I'd like to try describing my interpretation of Dorna through the images I've received. I was given rather complex three-dimensional visions that appeared up, down and sideways. Within the three-dimensional space lied several more three-dimensional worlds, all occupying the same space, but not in the same place; perhaps a fourth dimension. My head's spinning as I try to remember the details. The worlds are floating right pass each other, never really touching each other, but again, occupying the same space. In the three-dimensional space represented by Dorna, particles, when observed from the outside, are moving at a sluggish pace; but when they're observed from within the dimension, they're moving at a rapid pace. The Dorna dimension is lit by seven different spectrums of light – seven oceans all within one another. Each ocean has currents moving in all directions, never interacting with any other current or ocean. However, these currents as I understand them don't behave like normal ocean waves at all. I saw beams of light enter the dimensional Dorna from the parallel dimensions. The light that travels so fast outside the Dorna dimension comes to an almost screeching halt when it enters, while the opposite happens when the slow fluid light escapes Dorna, speeding back into parallel dimensions. Dorna's seven oceans are teeming with sparkles of light traveling up and down its currents. Some of those sparkles, I imagine, are spirits riding an ocean brimming with particle currents. The sparkles are similar in shade to the color of the ocean they swim in. Yet some sparkles can only swim in the one ocean with the color they share, while other sparkles can jump back and forth between the different oceans. I'm not sure if I'm getting it right, but by my understanding, some of the sparkles are oblivious to the existence of other oceans. It seems there's another three-dimensional world right below Dorna. It's a bit fuzzy and seems quite chaotic – an ocean of light, full of currents with no order or structure. Perhaps it's time for you to make sense of this.

You were shown a broad portrayal of Dorna's structure. Just like the physical casing in which it exists, Dorna consists of a visible three-dimensional landscape. However, one of the many things that sets Dorna apart from the other dimensions is the unique set of rules in which it operates. One of its unique properties, which we have not seen anywhere else in the vast universe, is its ability to interact with light particles in a way that slows them down and causes them to behave as if they were liquid. This phenomenon is the foundation of our existence, allowing us to travel at great speed (compared to your dimension) and in all directions as we please. Within this visible three-dimensional framework lies seen and unseen inner dimensions. The three-dimensional space you saw below Dorna is the passage. You are also right about the sparks. They are a representation of us spirits who traverse an ocean made of liquid light, doing what we do best, which is imagining and creating our own universe in a medium whose particles obey laws that may feel unfamiliar or unnatural to you.

You know what they'll say. That it's all nonsense. That there's no way any of this is true.

What would you rather believe: an afterlife of your own creation that allows you to advance further and sets you free on a path of your choosing, or an afterlife dictated by a gross misunderstanding of the chaotic passage and manipulated to serve as a means to an end? When we made the decision to tell you about our place, we took into consideration that there is no way for you to confirm our claims. We were never under the illusion that our words would become the official description of the afterlife. But if the scientific community (in particular the physicists and mathematicians) would integrate all they know using physics and math, they would discover not only that our existence and the world beyond are plausible, but also logical. We would also like to present another argument for why our description of Dorna is more grounded than any other group that ever gave a description of the afterlife. Anything positive requires work. Hard work. But the passive acceptance of beliefs, those reduced to following instructions in an already discovered understanding, requires no further effort or doing on the part of the believer.

As we describe Dorna to you, know that it is a place requiring hard work to further ourselves, which in turns translates to a positive result.

The science of quantum mechanics already takes us to weird and magical and mysterious worlds, so why not the world you describe?

Funny that you call it weird when, to us, your world is the weirdest.

How come?

The magic of plants growing. The vast variety of living things. The beauty of the physical world with its stars, planets, galaxies. Even when all are explained by science, it is still a purely magical thing.

You're fascinated with the physical world?

Aren't you?

It's joyful living on this planet. Even when you're down, I believe it's a blessing and a privilege to be alive. I know you've lived for a long time, but how far does your memory take you back?

Millions of Earth years. We originated from a simple, single, pure energy form. If we were to account for the time it took to go from the genesis of that energy form to the time we were able to maintain memories, then we have actually been alive for *billions* of years.

How do you know? After all, your memories only span millions *of years.*

Evolution takes its course in Dorna still today, even as we speak, in quite predictable ways. Spirits of the single, pure energy form are being born daily, and their evolution takes time. So, it is by observation that we know the history of where we came from and how long we have existed. Our origin is dictated by the same conditions as evolution in your world, but with one unique advantage: *our ability to control our evolution.*

So, you can evolve over there?

Not to the same extent as we did in the dimension that made us who we are today. We need the physical dimension, as we lack the fundamental ingredients a physical body provides.

Which is?

Confinement.

How?

Without confinement, there is no knowledge and no achievements.

Not following.

If you have the ability to climb a mountain effortlessly, you will never know the pain and suffering that comes with such feat. If you can hold your breath infinitely underwater, you will never know the discomfort of holding your breath for long. If you can run a marathon with ease, you will never know the toil it takes to prepare for such an achievement. None of this will ever give you joy if it is easily obtained. As we have said before, all good things are hard.

So, the afterlife is without confinements?

In many ways, yes. You would be surprised to learn that there are many spirits who do not take advantage of it.

If not all spirits take advantage of living in an unconfined space, does that mean you find yourself unique in this understanding?

Yes, this understanding is unfortunately limited to us alone for the time being. If most spirits who are longing for change would simply exercise their right to imagine and to release themselves from confinement, they could easily join us as well. It seems, however, that passing this threshold of freeing your mind is an endeavor not many are willing to take.

There's got to be a way of getting them to open their minds somehow.

There is a way. But not many are willing to take it. Perhaps we can use this time to send a message to them. A message with the hope of change.

And the message is?

Instead of wanting and expecting a change from others, you hold the power within you to initiate the change yourself. If you do not have what it takes to become the change, at least accept that others have a right to make their own change.

So, if one cannot change oneself alone, then by supporting others' right to change, one will eventually change anyway?

Support is a great thing, but it is more imperative that one believe others have the right to live freely. Believing in oneself as a unique individual, one that can create his own path – even if it is reserved to an inner belief visible only to the self – can help in freeing the mind in this life or even the next.

This may be out of place, but my mind is drifting to the way you travel in Dorna. You've explained a different method of travel from the first book we wrote. In "111 The Path," you told me you travel by thought, but now here, you say you ride on rays beaming through space!

It is one and the same. In fact, you travel by thought as well. Perhaps you travel differently than us physically, but any step you make still begins with a thought.

That is quite different. You told me you think of a place and you get there by thought. Yet for me to get there would mean I have to walk, drive or fly.

It is still travel by thought, only not instantaneous. There is no conflict or contradiction between the methods. Let us explain it better. Yes, we ride on beams of light by adjusting our subatomic particles. Every light beam has a different wave pattern (for reasons we are not going to mention right now). Every light beam is as unique as a snowflake. No one is the same as the other. By knowing the pattern of all beams on the way to our destination, we adjust our subatomic particles accordingly through the power of thought alone. The beams' patterns are like an address, a combination of ones and zeros that we remember, allowing us to travel across the patterns via our thoughts.

Which verifies what you've told me before: to travel by thought, you must know where you're going.

Exactly. And remember, we travel just below the speed of light, unable to violate the natural and absolute laws of God. While we are made of light particles and have the ability to harness great amounts of energy, we still contain mass. We are part of the building blocks of the universe. We are a part of God.

I want to go back to imagination for a moment. Let me see if I understand it. You can travel anywhere you want, yet you spend most of your time imagining. I can't even fathom all the places I would like to see using this ability.

What we have is the power of creation through the power of imagination. We make our own universe. In fact, you can do it as well. The only difference is that ours materializes instantaneously without the need for physical building blocks or financial planning. Imagine if your mind was able to manifest anything it imagined.

That would be the greatest power in the world.

Can you imagine how we feel possessing the power to create a universe just by thinking about it? And there is no one – no matter how powerful – who can put a cork on this ability. It is just unfortunate that this ability is within any spirit's grasp, yet the majority refuse to exercise it.

I must admit that sometimes I imagine my own universe, and it takes me far. If I was able to manifest it, wow, I would probably be the happiest person in the world! Just like dreams, at least those that I remember, imaginary worlds are these amazing experiences – even those that may be a bit uncontrollable or nightmarish.

Dreams are an uncontrollable manifestation of the soul. To most. There is actually a great connection between controlling an uncontrollable dream and being on the right path to becoming a great Pathian.

How can you control a dream?

By following the Pathian guidelines. We promise that controlling a dream is something anyone can master. It is the powerful connection of the soul with its spirit. It is magic that can be controlled just like a daydream.

Why are dreams so weird in nature?

Just because your dreams do not fit what you know in real life does not necessarily make them weird.

I agree with you on that. Not everything that is weird or unusual is wrong. You have to admit though that many dreams are purely and utterly bizarre. Why is that?

When the body is asleep, the soul is suspended between worlds inside the passage. It is a place where the soul finds it hard to control the power of imagination, a power which is a part of you in Dorna.

Why? Why is it so hard for the soul to control its imagination?

First, the soul is not settled within its spirit. Rather it is suspended inside the passage with no body to use as a medium for processing its consciousness, and therefore must do so via the passage itself. Second, in the passage, energy flows in curved lines, vortices and swirls. Imagine you are trying to shoot an arrow in a hurricane. The arrow would never shoot straight. Most likely, it would double back in your direction or go to the side or move in some other unpredictable way, no matter how many times you took aim. The passage (outside the intense flow of the opening tunnel to Dorna) is a complex array of light waves that flow in all directions, never following a straight line. Master the passage, and you become a better Pathian in any realm you are in.

Who would have known that by mastering my dreams, I master the passage, and by mastering the passage, I get better as a Pathian? But how is it that it's so weird? I still don't fully understand.

The passage is the soul's playground when the body is asleep. Being connected to the body has so many limitations, but the soul can exercise the unconfined ability of imagination using images related to the physical world when inside the passage. Creating a new reality for the soul to think and play in requires that it emit energy to its surroundings, which comes back to the soul to be processed again. The soul must use the passage as the medium for which thoughts are processed, just as it does with the brain when light bounces off objects into the eyes for the brain to process. The difference between the soul and the eye is that, in this case, the soul is also the originator of the light. This energy bounces off other particles of energy (as directed by the wishes of the soul) to be processed by the soul when it returns. Only in the passage, energy never moves as predictably as in Dorna or the physical world, causing the energy emitting from the soul to bounce around and return back for processing in an unorganized pattern, thereby creating an uncontrollable reality. Imagine if you saw the world with half your eye in the water and half outside it, getting a mixed wavelength of light interacting with the usual processes of the brain. Now, let's take it even further. All the light that originated at different times is not hitting your eyes at the same time, which means light waves that originated earlier may hit your eyes later than light waves that originated after. To make it simpler to understand, picture a dream where you are observing people walking on a street and the time is all mixed up. Past is in the present, present is in the future, and future is in the past. You see people walking in an unchronological timeframe. Now, to understand what the soul has to deal with inside the passage, multiply this description a thousand-fold. This is the perfect recipe for a night full of strange, uncontrollable dreams. Master this – master your dreams – and you can master *anything*. But to do so, you must master your *fears* first.

In the images you've shown me, the dimension right below what you describe as the afterlife is presumably a representation of the passage. A swirl of currents with no particular direction flowing in and out of other currents. A purely and utterly chaotic place with no logical order. No pattern whatsoever.

What you call a disorderly place we consider a place designated by God to fulfill our true purpose in mastering the one ability we can master freely: our imaginations. It is in this chaos that we refine the true nature of the soul.

Is it the chaotic state of the passage you mentioned earlier that further contributes to the confusion of the Earthbound spirits?

The passage is a place ruled by chaos. It is not enough that Earthbound spirits deprived of replenishing their energy have to deal with chaotic thoughts, unable to distinguish between truths and falsehoods. The closest representation of what an Earthbound spirit goes through is fatal familial insomnia, a rare disease causing panic attacks, paranoia, fear, rapid weight loss, dementia, and ultimately death. Earthbound spirits will not die, of course, but they will eventually lose any coherent purpose and drift into oblivion until saved.

So, the only way to tame the passage is through practice during sleep?

The nature of the passage cannot be tamed. It is the soul that must learn to overcome the difficulties of controlling its own thoughts and actions. It is the *soul* that must be tamed.

I think I have a subject that might fit into this line of questioning. I want to speak to you about a mental disorder.

Mental experience. Do not call it a disorder or disease. It is nothing but a great experience.

It's a bit harsh, don't you think, to call a mental disorder an experience? Look in their eyes, and you can see suffering and—

Harsh? Who is in charge of defining what is harsh? You, or anyone else for that matter, have no understanding of what they are going through to begin with. Suffering, you say? You are judging people with a disability from the perception of what you think a healthy body and mind should be. From our side, many of those you label mentally disturbed we consider to be great beneficiaries of the soul and our development.

The soul's development? How exactly can that state help the soul?

Their souls can traverse the passage as freely as they want, experiencing dreams that are unrestricted to sleeping periods. They are able to remain connected to the body and spirit, maintaining a consistent energy level at all times. Intense practice over a short period with many returns to the physical body would otherwise be required in order to get to the same level.

Can you at least explain what's going on?

The soul is in the body, but able to access the passage without the need for sleep. The passage puts the soul through a lot of challenges, inhibiting it from distinguishing the difference between the passage and the physical dimension. Nevertheless, the soul acts in accordance with its new reality, continuing to imagine and create. In the physical world, this behavior is viewed as if something is wrong with the person. Their inability to communicate and interact within the physical world, however, is not necessarily a disadvantage, especially when you have those who would take care of you.

But some would still call it abnormal.

Many would call them crazy. But do you think those who are in this state, those who are experiencing great adventures, care what people think about them?

Oh no, I don't doubt that for one second. They could care less about what people think of them. I wish those who didn't spend a lot of time in the passage would feel the same. So, do you choose this? Do you actually choose to experience this? Do you have a hand in creating such scenarios for yourself?

Yes. It is mostly done through self-choice. We have the ability to create certain conditions so the soul can later go through this amazing experience.

But why can't we intensify these experiences without affecting how the body behaves in the physical dimension?

Because we have yet to advance our ability to go through such experiences without causing the body this side effect.

What do you mean?

The contrast of the two worlds. The mediums by which we process our thoughts are different.

Explain.

Brain versus swirly space. The brain's thought process is familiar to you. It is what you call normal – using your senses to understand the outside world. But in the passage, the soul experiences thoughts in a much more chaotic manner, pulling from new senses on top of what the body offers. In fact, it is the freedom of the passage intertwined with the challenges of processing thoughts in a normal way that propels us faster in our understanding of the universe. That is why we encourage people to think outside the box, and by the box, we mean the brain. The fact that the soul thinks beyond the conventional constraints of the mind can cause it to behave in an unconventional way. We take advantage of this because a few thousand years back, we would not have survived long restricting this kind of experience to a short period.

The protection of the family permits this now. But how am I going to think outside my brain when I am confined to my body?

You are not confined to your body when you sleep or meditate or drift into a daydream, giving your soul the freedom to imagine so much of what it craves.

What's the reason a soul would seek to limit its interaction in this world while allowing it to navigate the passage freely?

Satisfaction. Practicing thoughts in a place full of challenges. Simple as that.

Should I inspire to do so as well? I mean aim to experience the passage in this way?

Not all need to. Not all want to. Some wish to advance in a faster way while some are already there. Some want a steady pace. We will give you a simple way to measure how advanced you are. It has to do with how you control the passage and your actions during the day. There is a lot more we need to discuss before we get there.

You told a story about the entrance to Dorna. I'm curious as to what kind of stories you tell in Dorna.

We tell stories about a soul venturing into the physical world, hoping to make a change and influencing others to change as well so transformation will become easier. We tell of all the hardship he endures while trying to achieve this change. We tell of how this spirit must abandon all that he knows again and again just so he can gain new knowledge in pursuit of new levels. We tell—

This tale feels like it's about me.

You are one of them. But you are not the only one this tale speaks of. It is a tale for all who feel a disconnect from the norms of society. They are your children, family members, friends, neighbors and co-workers.

I wanted a unique tale.

We are not sure any story we would tell would make sense to you. We can definitely tell you a story of the Earth / Heaven connection, but it will not be short. It is a story about greatness and lowness, filth and lushness, evilness and kindness, cleanliness and brutality, an end and a beginning, a story that would never take place, a story that opens doors to who knows what. This is not a story for one paragraph; it is a story for a book. It is a story we can share with you once our message has been delivered.

Fair enough. Earlier, you spoke of God's breath flowing through you, getting stronger as you advance, but I don't remember seeing anything in the images that would indicate God's energy other than those oceans of light.

That is because we are unable to describe such energy, even through an image. It is an energy unlike anything else in the universe. It is an energy that defines us in ways that cannot be explained.

Why can't it be explained?

Because it is never the same. It is different for each and every one of us. Perhaps we shall speak of this later as the description of Dorna becomes clearer.

In the images I've seen, there are seven oceans within Dorna. Seven is a number that repeats itself quite often in places like the Bible, the Quran, and many other religious texts. Why is it that the images you've chosen to show contain seven oceans?

It is the number of planes that can currently be seen by us in Dorna. There are currently only seven planes of awareness.

Chapter 5

Planes of Awareness

I once read a concept that said we are here on Earth to align ourselves with God, and in so doing, we uplift the heavens. Does that make any sense to you?

Yes. It is what we do. Uplifting the heavens. Uplifting it beyond the seventh plane.

What are these "planes" you speak of?

Planes, levels, realms – they are all one and the same. We speak of hidden planes of awareness, hidden knowledge, which you gain with each step as you advance. Aligning ourselves with our Creator, we push ourselves up. Or rather forward. We align ourselves with God.

Let's start from the beginning, please. What are these levels of awareness? Can you explain it in terms I'll understand?

Currently in Dorna, there are seven hidden and visible planes. We use both terms – hidden and visible – to describe them, because it is true from both perspectives. The only way to see a plane is to align yourself with its vibration.

And how do you that?

By making a change to the spirit through the body in the physical world.

Okay, I'm really getting confused here. Seven levels. Hidden, but visible. Alignment with the Creator. You've got to make a bit more sense. How can a level be visible and hidden at the same time?

Each level of visibility becomes apparent when the spirit advances in its development, positioning it higher and thereby allowing it to gain knowledge it would not otherwise be able to gain. Perhaps it is time for an analogy. And an apology. We sometimes forget that what is clear to us is not so clear to others. That said, in continuing the analogy of the climber, we would like you to imagine a tower with floors made of one-way mirrors. Each floor's mirrors have the reflective surface facing down, which means a person can see the floors below by looking down, but will only see their own reflection on the ceiling when they look up. Anyone on the first floor is oblivious to the second floor because they cannot see anything beyond the mirror's reflection. The second-floor occupants see things a little differently. They likewise cannot see through their ceiling, and therefore assume there is nothing above them, but when they look down, they can see the occupants from the first floor very clearly. Occupants on the third floor can see those on the second floor and the first floor, and so on and so forth until you get to the seventh floor. Those at the top can naturally see the most. They see all the way down to the first floor.

Quite a vantage point. So, each floor is both visible and hidden depending on what level you're situated on.

Yes.

What floor are you on?

We are on the seventh. You are on the seventh. The tower is just another analogy, like the mountains we always refer to. We aim to move forward, to see a bit more beyond the next peak.

I understand why we aim to move forward, but I don't understand how this all actually works in your world. How exactly does the tower of one-way mirrors work in your dimension?

Our true tower operates completely differently than what we describe, of course. In our tower, the floors have connected elevators that vibrate on different levels which, depending on your location, allow you to go below and back. It is only by the effort of the soul making a change to the spirit through an active change of the body that our energy is able to vibrate and adjust freely to any plane that is visible to us, giving us insight into different elements of our universe and a better understanding of who God is, who we are.

Sounds like a mess. But I think I'm getting it.

To further complicate your understanding, we must also tell you that even though our sight can go all the way to the seventh plane, our spirit and our body remain visible within the spirit realm at all planes.

So, if I'm getting this right, you're saying you can see beyond the mountains without ever leaving the valley.

Yes. Every floor, every plane comes with new understanding, a new view of the world. Take the sunset in your world. We are all aware that the sun setting on the horizon happens every day. We all agree on that. But in the tower, the sunset is seen first on the first floor and last on the top floor due to the curvature of the earth. So, a person watching the sunset from the first floor who does not have access to the floors above will disagree with the claims from people who are on the top floors that the sun has yet to set and would pointlessly argue whether it has set or not.

So, in accordance with our discussions in the first book, we're trying to bring more Pathians onto the seventh plane?

No. We are trying to push *beyond* the seventh plane, but it inevitably requires more souls traversing the seventh.

But you cannot see any other plane beyond the seventh.

In the tower, the occupants of the first through the sixth floors are in denial that other floors exist above them. It is the argument that prevents them from ever reaching it. As for us, we cannot ignore the possibility that simply because we cannot see them, planes do not exist above us. It is just a simple matter of progression; we have yet to replicate beyond the seventh plane.

So, what's the problem? Let's figure out how to align our bodies, as you say, in the physical dimension and push through this change in the afterlife.

It is not that easy. To affect the change we seek, we must increase our numbers. Our change is reliant on many people reaching and aligning with the seventh plane.

I'm going to sound like my son when he was a young child, and I'm probably going to repeat this question as much as he did. Why?

We will explain it more thoroughly when we speak on how we travel to the physical dimension, but for now, imagine that you have made a change to the soul and are now situated in the seventh plane. We will use the analogy of a 30-foot wall to describe the obstacle separating you from the eighth plane. In our scenario, you have no tools at your disposal. How will you get to the eighth plane?

How am I going to do that? Let's see. I have no tools and jumping wouldn't do me any good. It's simply too high unless you can jump 30 feet in the afterlife. But then again, the analogy takes place in my world, so I guess I'm stuck.

Would you maybe ask for someone's help? Perhaps someone could give you a push? But wait, one more person would not do you any good either. Even if you had several weak people to help you, it would not do you any good. What you need is more *strong* people like yourself who can lift a person on their shoulders. When you have enough of these people, you can create a human ladder, taking you beyond the wall into the eighth plane.

And these strong people, where do I find them?

Well, here, they are easily recognizable. Their presence is easily felt. But they are fairly recognizable in your world as well. Imagine the feat they must undertake to get to the top. Those who do so are quite qualified to give the push required. In fact, those who wish to give you that push you so desire are just as curious and motivated to reach beyond as you are. But like you, they must wait their turn, wait for more capable people such as them to give them a push beyond the wall. This is the cycle we must increase. The good thing about reaching the eighth plane is that once you are there, you can guide those from the lower levels. We believe that once a soul has insight into the eighth plane, what it sees will be valuable to all.

And this insight cannot be gained while you're within the seventh plane?

No. Can you tell what lies beyond a mountain range? Is it another mountain range? Is it a valley? Is it a desert? Is it an ocean? Perhaps a lake? How about what plants and animals live beyond? Are there new elements in there? Are God's laws different there? These are questions that can only be answered when viewed directly. For us, it is like a zap of knowledge gained in an instant the minute the spirit body is exposed to it. This zapping of information is what we long for.

I understand now. We need more people to change their ways so they will be able to tune their spirit to see into the seventh plane, thereby giving a collective push that will align our bodies with the vibration of the eighth plane. Then, we can gain instantaneous insight into the workings of our Creator, which I assume is a great experience.

That is true.

And living our life the Pathian way will help us do so.

We believe so. It has worked thus far. There is no reason it would stop.

I can't help but repeat myself. How could it be that the Earth, the physical dimension, is the place to advance oneself spiritually through the planes? What's the logic in this? Why would we rely on this place?

It is this question that drives us further in our understanding, and the fact is that with our current abilities, the physical dimension is the only path that allows us to advance. Why is it this way? Today, we are simply not sure. Would we want to know it all, with no need to advance? What would be the purpose of life then? This is good. A journey through an uncharted territory is amazing. To us, the Earth is a tool; an anchor attached to a rope that allows us to throw it over the cliffs so we can climb beyond our obstacles.

The Earth is a tool.

A great tool. A tool many have passed on using. But not us. We recognize this tool's ability to shape our destiny and we have no intention of passing on it. To the contrary, we shall exhaust every tool at our disposal just to acquire one more piece of information about what we are a part of.

Where are these seven planes? Are they like the tower, one on top of the other?

No. They are one *within* the other, sharing the same space. It is an ocean of light within an ocean of light, just as you have seen.

Why not speak to the spirits in the lower levels and tell them of the great views, wonders and understandings beyond their existence so perhaps they would be encouraged to push forward and get there?

There is a problem. A spirit body whose sight can penetrate the seventh level remains visible to all occupants of all levels. This in itself causes many from the lower levels to doubt the validity of our claims, negating their interest in pursuing anything other than the status quo. Unable to see beyond their limited realm means they refuse to believe us. Even those who know for a fact that there are levels below them are reluctant to believe anything continues beyond what their sight allows them to see. It is perplexing how one who has experienced change refuses to believe there can be more changes beyond that simply because they cannot find the way. It mystifies us that only when we get to the seventh plane does this understanding come so naturally.

It doesn't make much sense. They can obviously see levels beneath them, yet they preclude the possibility that other higher levels exist. Regardless, some spirits do wish to continue aligning themselves with God; otherwise, there wouldn't be any other levels to speak of.

That is true. There are always exceptions. The problem is that the higher up you move, the lonelier it gets, and it has been this way for a long time. There are not many who speak of the view from the seventh plane. It is what we wish to change.

I understand that to move up the levels, we must make the change here, but how does this change actually allow you to see more planes?

The spirit body is like an expandable sail. It is quite adaptable to change. The soul is transformed through the body. Those changes allow our expandable sail to increase its interacting surface, not by increasing the sail's surface size per se, but rather through our ability to adjust the distance between our molecules. Now, we must differentiate between the molecules that allow us to travel upon the light and the molecules that allows us to capture God's energy. The constant expansion and contraction of what we refer to as God's particles made through His energy interacting with nothing allows us to interact with more energy, thereby allowing us to tune into higher planes.

Then you are a different breed from lower level spirits made by your own evolutionary process.

Yes, we are. But it is not something that is unique only to us. Anyone from any level can evolve, perhaps even faster, and we are here to lend a guiding hand.

You say that a spirit's level is easily identifiable in the afterlife. I was wondering if there's a way to identify at what level a person's spirit belongs right here in the physical dimension?

There is. You can easily identify a human's soul level by the characteristics of a person, which is an indication of their current evolutionary progress.

But how? What characteristics define the levels?

There are questions one can ask, and the answers will reveal the characteristics associated with each plane. We can help you to create a series of questions that allow individuals to identify where they belong. We believe this tool can help identify the needed changes a soul must practice. Just to mention a few: Do you ask questions? Are you easily influenced? Are you a follower or a leader? Are you a good listener? Do you get upset easily? Are you intimidated by others? Are you open-minded? *Truly* open-minded? Do you believe in God?

That would definitely be interesting. I think a way to identify a person's level can help in identifying the area needing the most change. Changes are so hard in the physical dimension, but we need to evolve to gain access to the eighth plane.

We are not only about gaining access to the eighth plane. We want to reach *beyond* it. God's particle vibrations have only been slight, and yet we were able to access the seventh level. Within the full span of those molecules' vibrations... Ah, our imagination is not sufficiently developed to take us there. You are wrong about change being hard though. It is as hard as you make it out to be. Or as easy as you make it out to be.

Do you think I'm capable of this feat? Of reaching the eighth plane?

Perhaps. It can definitely happen. It is something we wish for any one of us at the seventh plane. But to continue on your trip, you cannot do it alone. We rely on the help and advancement of other spirits from lower levels.

Let's assume someone goes through these questions. Of course, that person would have to be as truthful as possible for the results to be reliable. Now let's assume one finds out, in accordance with his answers, that he belongs in the fourth plane. Is it possible for him to make a single leap from the fourth all the way to the seventh?

Anything is possible. But it is not going to be easy. It requires hard work and practice. There is a reason a person finds himself at a certain level. It is easier when the leap is done in stages. To give you an example, a person with a jealous temperament cannot transform his behavior in a single shot. Nevertheless, it is not impossible, as traumatic events foisted upon a person can transform his personality in a single moment. Unfortunately, not only are those traumatic events rare, but a lot of times, they do not work.

If only people knew the right way to live.

People do know what the right way to live is. It surprises us that someone so ready to give advice to others on most occasions does not live by it himself. We see that everywhere. There is a great difference between what people say and what they do.

I agree with you. I see it all the time. You look at intelligent people who study and know quite a lot, but when it comes to practice, they're incapable. Then there are others who do not study as much, but in practice are like hungry lions set upon prey. When looked at this way, I would much rather be the hungry lion.

There is so much you will learn from practice that books will never give you. It is sad that many think knowledge alone without practice is the be-all and end-all of human existence.

Do you think that one day through the vibration of God's particles we will finally get to be closer to God? And I don't mean like sitting with Him or talking to Him, but rather understanding Him completely?

We do not think it will ever happen. The assumption is that to get to God, He must stand still. And He does not. He is evolving just as we are through His creations. However, as Pathians, we never say never. We would prefer to think that as we get closer to understanding Him, God in His own way would look upon us with a smile, not saying a word – a smile that says finally some of My creations have figured out the path. It would be a smile of accomplishment.

Where does this drive to understand God, to evolve, come from?

We are a part of God. We are made of His particles. It is our duty and privilege to enhance the powers that were given to us. We refuse to believe that such powers were only given to test our ability at fighting temptation. A creator creates. A creator gives freedom to create. A creator wants to see his creation grow. It is what He is and it is what we are supposed to be.

As a Pathian, I'd like to throw a curve ball at you. What if there is no eighth level? What if level seven is all there is?

It is not a possibility. Our energy, the way we are made, simply precludes any conceivable notion that there is nothing beyond, and therefore we are unable to perceive such a possibility.

I'd like to ask you another question, and then I'll take you back to the one I just asked. How is it that all religions coincidently speak of seven as some important number? Islam speaks of seven dimensions, yet nothing in their practices is even remotely close to the way of the Pathian. Christianity speaks of opening seven seals, which sounds similar to passing through the seven levels. Not to mention Judaism, whose number seven represents so many aspects of their beliefs. Is the constant mentioning of the number seven in Islam, Judaism and Christianity the seven levels of awareness you speak of? Moreover, do the seven planes influence Jewish beliefs in this mystical number?

One and the same.

Then how do you explain their interpretations?

Have you already forgotten what we discussed in the first book? How the interpretation of what was once revealed has perverted its true meaning? Our previous efforts to speak to souls who were incapable of understanding us has in a way backfired on us. You cannot teach someone to run before they learn to walk. It is hard to change a person just by telling them, even if the tellings are from beyond their world. It is a bit frustrating, but because of our effort to evolve and understand, we have shifted our efforts in the direction we take now.

I share your frustration. It's hard to change people, in particular those who are faithful to their beliefs without even knowing the root cause that put them there to begin with. You ask them for the origin of their beliefs, which is almost always their upbringing. When I think, what if they ask me the same question, I realize my answer would be quite simple. Because I know God.

The root cause?

I feel Him. Not because I was told to. Not because of a book. Not because I'm afraid. Not because I'm trying to fit in. But through my questions and my continuously evolving journey. I'll never have proof for the many. The proof is for me alone through my own doing.

Exactly.

It dawned on me that the actual place you speak of – the seventh plane – is in fact the seventh heaven so spoken of by Judaism and Islam. Similar, yet not the same. How could it be?

Out of our stories, they manage to manifest a perceived description of where we are – a state of bliss, a state of great joy, a state of satisfaction. It is unfortunate that they have put chains on every possibility and every path and every gate that can lead them into the seventh heaven they so fervently believe in. It is no coincidence that most religions speak of seven heavens or seven obstacles in the afterlife. The fact forever remains that the knowledge of the seven planes has been available to all from the time we were aware of them. Yet even with that knowledge, it has eluded them that such simple actions like following the true meaning of the natural and absolute laws of God (in particular, the Ten Commandments) can and will lead them to the actual realm they are so desperate to reach.

Why would spirits on the planes not ask about or seek higher planes? What do they have to lose?

They are afraid of retribution from stating their opinion. Fear causes them to follow, and as such, they fail to exercise their right to imagine.

It's hard for me to understand the fear of stating your mind, of believing in something that's not common. I can't imagine living a life where I only say or act the way I'm "supposed to." After all, it's only words and beliefs. I'm not hurting anyone. My brain is faster than my speech. I'd compare it to the passage, which sometimes causes my words to come out differently than I intended. I can make people laugh with funny punchlines, but sometimes, either because of my accent or rapid thinking, I've been known to mess up a good joke or punchline, leaving my friends unsure of what to make of it. The truth is that the thought of sounding silly doesn't really occur to me, nor does it bother me much. I know who I am, and my friends never lead me to believe that such verbal missteps would be a reason for avoiding me. I believe that regardless of who you are, you should never be afraid to speak your mind, never be afraid to be different, especially if you're living in a place that holds democracy dear.

You should never be afraid. You are right about another thing as well.

What's that?

You do know how to mess up a good joke.

I think this is the first time you've ever showed a sense of humor... Okay, so at what level are religious believers situated?

One of the basic principles that enable us to vibrate at a higher level is a free mind – one that is able to conceive of a higher understanding. The second most important thing is our uniqueness, our individuality, which separates us from the followers. Following robs you of being unique and places you, at best, on the third plane. Religious followers' inability to develop their uniqueness has stagnated them for many, many years.

I ask this question because I want to know how many levels it would take for them to advance. Do different religions have different positions? What I'm trying to get at is, do Jews, Muslims and Christians all share the same plane, or are their mitigating factors that might situate them differently on different planes?

It does not work that way. Your plane is not based on your religion, but rather manifests itself based on the limitation of your beliefs and abilities. The planes care less whether you are Muslim, Jewish, Christian, Hindu, or any other religion that exists on the face of the Earth. What it does care about are the elements that limit your spiritual growth, which are the same elements that limit all religions without exception, including non-religious persons who by self-virtue limit their own beliefs.

So, if I limit myself through any mechanism, I—

Shall find yourself trapped under the same conditions.

How does it work?

The planes are all there for you. Through zero limitations, you can acquire the tools that will allow you to penetrate the very thing that prevents others from doing so.

I still don't get it.

Imagine you are about to walk through a barrage of obstacles to reach different levels. To reach the first level, you must pass through a sand storm. To reach the second level, you must cross a river infested with man-eating piranhas. To reach the third level, you must cross a forest on fire. At every point prior to encountering the obstacle, you can do things that will enable you to access a tool. Prior to the first level, you can earn sand storm goggles. How do you earn them? For the sake of this metaphor, let's say you must jump 50 times. Now, among you, there are those who believe it is a sin to jump more than 10 times, while others think jumping 50 times is simply impossible, and therefore won't even try. In addition, there is a little catch.

Which is?

You must do the jumping alone and of your own free will without any coercion by others. If you can follow those simple rules, then by completing the first task of jumping 50 times, you will find in your possession a pair of sand storm goggles – visible to you, but invisible to everyone else – prior to undertaking the first level journey. Now you find yourself with a tool that allows the obstacle to be an obstacle no more and, moreover, allows you to forever move back and forth between the lower and higher level reached. The same idea applies to the rest of the levels. Prior to the second level, you notice that you are cut off by a river of man-eating piranhas, and the tool you must earn is a wooden boat. Only now, the task that you must complete to earn this boat is a bit harder (and one that we shall leave to your imagination). Once you have reached the second level, you again encounter a new obstacle – the fire forest – and will need to master yet another new task to gain another promised tool that shall remain hidden until earned, but is guaranteed to provide safe passage through the flames. In real life, the barriers are invisible and the tasks are unknown, yet we have learned that by diminishing the physical body's and soul's limitations adhering to the natural and absolute laws of God, we are able to breach the planes with the acquired new tools. To make it easy on you, look at your world and tell us what you see. You are limited to a world that your mind can comprehend through your senses; however, you know there is more to it even if you cannot see it, because today, through science, you are able to reveal details that are hidden. For instance, if you were watching a rainbow a thousand years ago, you would know it contained seven colors because the human eye has three color receptors – red, green and blue – and each of them will respond to a small section of the spectrum. But if you were told that beyond what you can see, with no tools to prove it, there are other colors that you cannot see due to the limitations of the human eye, you would likely doubt it. Today, you know that beyond red is "infrared" and beyond violet is "ultraviolet," which can only be seen using a tool. But what if we told you that in that rainbow and all around you are many more colors than you can see, a condition which can be changed if only you advance sufficiently in your understanding of God's creation, allowing you to acquire the tool needed to give you the necessary sight?

You know what they'll say. That we're heading in the wrong direction. In their eyes, where they're at is the only place to be. Anywhere else is just asking for trouble. They'll say the eighth dimension you speak of is not a place of growth, but rather a place of torment. Fire and brimstone. A place where Hell exists. In fact, I would derive that some would consider the passing of the seventh plane as the opening of the seventh seal as described in the Book of Revelation. Once breached, it would bring about the end of time, the Apocalypse.

This is not new, as they have said this before. They said this would happen when we ventured beyond the fifth. When we told them we can see beyond the fifth, they did not believe us. They said that on the sixth we would reach Hell. Today, we agree that the story will only repeat itself, and the eighth, as far as we are concerned, would be no different.

How do you explain it then? That the further you go up the planes, the less religious you become?

Imagine that right on the first plane sits a temple of worship. Spirits who are confined of their own accord to the first plane are oblivious to the other planes and all they can see is this temple. The temple becomes an inseparable part of them. If you manage to climb up the planes, you will see not only the temple, but more. You can see beyond. And as such, this new reality will give rise to more questions and the need to further satisfy your own curiosity. The higher you rise on the planes, the less significant your contribution to one plane. The temple of worship we speak of is an inescapable behavioral pattern prevalent within the first few planes, and those who wish to reach higher will always remain connected to the bottom, pulled by its immense effect.

Let me see if I understand this right. If the lower planes that are connected to religious behavioral patterns one day disappear, we'll be able to advance a bit faster by eliminating the part that's holding us all back, eventually making the lower planes nonexistent.

The lower planes will never dissolve. They may be low from where we are, but spiritual beings who have not taken the form of humans yet look upon them as desirable destinations because they are upper planes of existence. They are planes that will forever have an influence on us, drawing us lower. It is our job to move forward; to move beyond their strong grip; to move to a place where it is no more a thorn in our side that adversely affects our development.

Aren't you afraid of the unknown?

Yes, we are. We have yet to master this feeling, but our curiosity and obligation outweigh the fear easily.

What if there is possible danger lurking within the next plane?

Then another question arises. What is lurking beyond that danger? We cannot allow fear to shape who we are. We would rather allow curiosity to be the force that keeps us moving. Curiosity and imagination know no boundaries.

Since you don't like the word "disorder" to describe those who we consider mentally impaired, I will phrase my next question carefully. At what levels are those who experience the passage with greater ease while retaining the body situated?

The highest currently known. The seventh plane. They have helped us in understanding The Path more than any other.

Do you have more energy than other spirits? In other words, does a spirit on the seventh plane have more energy than one who is on the first?

Yes. This increased energy is what allows us to tune and vibrate at higher rates; but there is a side effect to this, albeit not necessarily a negative one. The further up we get in the levels, the further we distance ourselves from the physical dimension. It is this phenomenon that tells us, at some point further up, there will be no need for us to return to the physical dimension to make the change needed. We believe that, eventually, our spiritual body will evolve far enough so as to continue the change from within Dorna. This distancing, though, makes it harder to open the communication channels between us and you, thereby enhancing the importance of our communications today.

Am I to understand that lower levels can communicate with a greater ease than you?

Yes. That surprises you?

Yes. I assumed that the more energy you have, the more things you can actually do. And communicating with us would be one of those things. But now you tell me otherwise.

Did it ever occur to you why there are always four of us?

To be honest, no, it never crossed my mind. In my own imaginative way, I assumed you wished to make it symbolic of my "forefathers."

No symbolism whatsoever. It is our combined energy that allows us to open a communication channel between us and you. Alone, this would be impossible.

Why? It doesn't make sense.

Imagine a mountain…

Again with the mountain?

Entertain us. Imagine yourself climbing a mountain with your friends. In order to communicate with the base camp located at the bottom, you can easily shout to convey a message. But as you climb higher, you find that your shouting brings no answers. It is at this point that you may ask your friends to combine their efforts and yell aloud together, which carries more energy, thus allowing the sound to travel further down to the base. The further you climb, the more experience you get, and the more experience you get, the more distant you find you are from others. This is part of our evolution. You can be at the bottom, experience nothing, but communicate with ease; or you can be at the top, experience all there is, but suffer on the other end.

What happens when you can no longer communicate with us?

Perhaps it is part of our evolution that at some point in time, we will no longer depend on a physical body. Maybe we will all find ourselves beyond the seventh plane, free from the constraints of advancement through your world. As Pathians, of course we must admit this is just a theory, albeit one that all evidence concludes must exist.

I'd very much like to continue testing this theory.

That is what we are working on.

Speaking of which, are all spirits able to communicate with us? All spirits of all levels?

Spirits from all levels can communicate with you, but that is not to say that every spirit has the ability to communicate. Actually, it is quite uncommon for individual spirits to be able to do so. It is a talent you either have or you do not.

The reason I ask is that many mediums who claim to speak to spirits tell of a different message than the one you're telling me. Some messages are peaceful, some are of a religious nature, and some are even malicious. Is it perhaps that their communicators are speaking to them from a different plane, a different point of view?

This is Dorna, a place with a multitude of realities and messages. We ask that you listen to none, including ours. Never rely on any message as the definitive truth. Be your own judge of what is right and what is wrong and—

They scare you? Their messages scare you?

Their messages terrify us. It is a chokehold on the freedom of the mind. It is a continuous barrier that we constantly must cross. If only they had a clearer understanding of the universe and God that spanned through all levels, we would have effortlessly been able to advance.

Do you think there could be some spirits who've already crossed to the eighth plane?

No spirit has yet to cross.

How can you be so sure? Could it be that there are already spirits who have traversed the eighth plane, and you're not even aware of it?

We are all connected in ways we cannot explain, but know that any addition to our count is felt and any reduction to our count is also felt. Think of us as an air tank under pressure. Any additional air will increase the pressure and speed of molecular vibration, thereby also changing the temperature. If an air molecule represents a spirit, then an increase in the speed of vibration and subsequent rise in temperature would indicate additional air molecules in the tank, just as a reduction in vibration and subsequent cooling would indicate fewer air molecules. Our senses act quite similarly to the behavior of air molecules, which allow us to feel the subtlest changes going this way or that. We have felt this sensation as spirits moved from one plane to the other, but all are accountable. We have yet to see a reduction that has no traceability. And in case this analogy does not sit right with you, know that we are all part of God's universal consciousness. Every action that is done within this consciousness affects us, rendering any change noticeable.

But how can you sense across so many planes and so many spirits? There are probably several billion spirits hanging out in the afterlife, and it's not as if you do a head count of each soul, do you?

Some senses are beyond your understanding. We are so sensitive in this way, that we can perceive the most minute sensation, one that would indicate subtle changes to our state that negate the need to conduct a head count.

What makes you think there will be an eighth plane?

Continuity pattern. When there was only one plane visible, one reality, no one thought there was more. Yet as a consequence of our behavior, a second plane opened up, and then a third, and so on. Some of us recognized a pattern through trial and error, through our ability to break old patterns as we went along. We were able to establish unique universal principles that allowed us to advance and become better married with the universe, with God. Today, we have seven planes (visible to some at least), and within higher planes the understanding that there is no end to how high we can go. However, the patterns that held us back remain by our side at all times. You see, when there was only one plane, and then two, and so on, there were always those who said, "This is it, there are no more."

There are always those who choose stagnation for reasons that are beyond me.

Because of our ability to create change and overcome stubbornness, the eighth plane shall become a reality very soon.

Now that we understand the purpose of our existence, how do we change? I have a feeling this change must be a book in and of itself.

This time, it will just be a chapter. And this time, we will not discuss how to change per se, but rather the arguments in favor of change and the implications when it is lacking. There will be a time when we dedicate a whole book to address the question of how. Whatever awaits us in the eighth plane and beyond is a mystery we must reveal. The preparation takes place in the physical world, and for that, we must prepare. We start with the power of change.

Chapter **6**

The Power of Change

Do we all have the power to change?

Yes.

I'm still trying to wrap my head around the idea that changes done here will influence my spiritual body over there. Regardless of the eventual benefits we reap over there, I think we can first benefit from the changes right here.

Absolutely. And the beauty of it is that while you may enjoy the fruit of your change in the physical realm, the benefit that awaits you in Dorna will be felt a hundred-fold. But for that, you must become a Pathian.

Not everybody can start the change that way though. Not everyone is born a Pathian.

Every soul, no matter where it is born or from which plane it has descended, is born a Pathian. It is the natural way we journey through the physical world. Unfortunately, as we grow, we tend to slip away from this natural course due to the influence of those who came before us. However, as far as you may slip away, it is rather easy to return. A Pathian can come from any spectrum of the world. Some were raised as Jews, others as Christians, some as Muslims and others as Buddhists. What sets any person on the return journey to once again becoming a Pathian is the simple act of asking a question. This simple act will grow with time, multiplying via the asking of further questions that eventually will reveal the truth and allow the asker to mature out of his religion, out of his limiting environment, and back into what he was once comfortable with. It requires but a simple act of daring, to ask, to seek, daring in spite of those who will try to contain him and fill his heart with fear.

I identify with what you're saying. I sometimes find myself alone in my understanding of how things are. I see discussions about politics or world events, and while most stand on one side agreeing wholeheartedly with the tastemakers, I find that my opinion is often quite different. And it is only when I state my opinion that I find I'm not alone. Others wait, I suppose, for a braver soul to speak prior to stating their mind for fear of retribution. How do we face this? How do we fight this fear?

When the time comes, we will give you the knowledge and power so you can rise above. For now, you can start by not being a sheep led by the shepherd.

It's funny that you speak of the shepherd and the sheep. I've been pondering this same principle for a long time. It's weird to me that most religions keep using the word shepherd to mean leading. "I am your shepherd." This is an opportunity for me to vent my feelings on the subject. While others use this word to symbolize the greatness of one person who comes and saves us all, where exactly is my part *in all of this? What exactly am I? A* sheep. *Sheep are hapless, defenseless creatures, and it's very rare to see a sheep living outside the group, as they require the constant protection of the shepherd. They graze most of the day, moving in unison, bundled together not by ideology, but by the instinct for protection. The sheep that religions refer to were tamed by man. Is this what God meant for me to be? Something to be tamed by Him? To huddle up like a defenseless creature with only a superior being to protect me? Is this how ancient humans saw themselves? No wonder I don't seem connected. But if I must be a sheep, then let it be a wild sheep climbing over hills and mountains, living free within a small group, able to avoid predators (without the need of a shepherd), moving from one place to another freely. And though they're still following the mature ram, they're free to leave any time they want, unlike the domestic sheep that will be carried or pushed back if they try to stray. I think another quality that prevents religion from ever using a wild sheep in their analogy is that wild sheep must often flee uphill when detecting predators, but will fight back when necessary. They have very keen senses of sight and hearing, which are heightened as a result of their freedom. This is one of those moments that gets me upset about the delusional world of religion.*

You know the truly scary part? The tamed sheep started out just like the wild sheep, as intended by God. It will not be long before the contrasting elements of their past are erased. Erased by humanity, never by God. We cannot allow this to happen to us, which is why we need to push further away from religion's influence. We must rise to higher levels where this influence is merely faded background noise; where we can easily navigate around it. We must become a solid rock able to withstand the force of the floods, yet light enough to rise above it.

An interesting analogy of two opposite characteristics for a rock.

We are operating from a world where opposites coexist quite comfortably with each other.

If only it were possible here.

By the way, did you notice that you used a mountain in your description of the sheep?

Yes, I did. I guess you've been rubbing off on me. I've seen so many sheep and lambs led around the hillside of my former country, and that's not the image I have in mind for myself or for anyone else. It frustrates me that not many see it this way. How can we turn people away from being led and toward being leaders? How can we inspire them to climb the ladder of the planes?

You can spread the word. Raise your voice. Write a book.

But then again, change is not easy. Those who need it the most don't even know they need it. As far as they're concerned, they're perfectly fine just the way they are. How will they see the truth that lies before them?

We are not saying it is going to be easy. We are not arrogant enough to think we can change everyone. But those who reach out, those who dare to ask questions, are who we seek. As for the others, we will have to understand them better prior to helping them.

How?

Have you ever heard of the Dunning-Kruger effect?

No.

The Dunning-Kruger effect is a term that was recently given to a phenomenon that has existed for eternity, whereby unskilled, uninformed people will tend to overestimate the level of their skills and knowledge. They suffer from an illusory superiority that makes them unable to recognize their lack of skill. In our case, people are so arrogant as to think they have figured it all out when so much is left to learn.

I've met those people. They frustrate me greatly. They tend to preach based on a false illusion of knowledge. They believe they're liked, and they can't comprehend the extreme heights of their inadequacy. Here are my problems. When I converse with people who think they know basically everything, I usually don't want to listen to them. You can say whatever you wish to them, even the opposite of what they say, and they won't bother to take notice. Sometimes I stay silent around those people. I keep my thoughts to myself. I don't participate. I feel it's a waste of my time and energy to engage in an argument, even if I can easily obtain proof of my position. Should I engage with a person who would fail to recognize that they are victims of the Dunning-Kruger effect?

You engage in an argument only if you can back it up with proof. We have seen throughout our existence that arguments with no solid evidence to back them up will have no effect. In this day and age, you must prove your argument. If you cannot, stay silent. The Dunning-Kruger effect shows that when people recognize their faults after being repeatedly exposed to facts, they eventually will change.

You're asking me to prove to people through facts that they're incompetent?

We ask that you prove them wrong without leaving any doubt. Back up your ideas with as much proof as possible. As an example, many use false data to prove that Noah and the Great Flood took place by giving evidence of the existence of his ark. They point to an archeological site and artifacts that are in fact not real. They then spread this misinformation, giving false legitimacy to its existence with no refutation on the same scale. And since we speak of how to change oneself in this chapter, know that by raising those facts and engaging those who wish to ask, you help them to change, help them to realize that their incompetence robs them of the ability to realize the truth.

I know a man who thinks of himself as a great speaker. He believes he can mesmerize people with his tales, while in fact he bores them to death. When you look at the listeners' faces, you can see them shift their heads to the side and, little by little, look for an excuse to get away. All of this happens right in front of him, and what I see he can see as well. But he doesn't. I believe this person is the epitome of the Dunning-Kruger effect. That even when he can't keep the crowd interested, he still remains confident in his ability as a storyteller. Now, how am I supposed to help a person like that? Do I tell him? The first thing he'll think is that I'm being cruel or jealous. I have some advice for him, but I know he won't take it the right way. He is, after all, the very definition of a "know-it-all."

Do you want to help him? Do you want to see him do better?

Yes.

Then back up your claims with facts. Use your words carefully. Show that your intent is to provide support. Most people do not like to be criticized, even if the criticism is constructive.

But real facts backed by evidence and compassion can and will enlighten a person, even if it looks harsh at the beginning. One must truly admit his own limitations and faults before one can improve. The good thing is that we are just like arrows. Sometimes we need to be held back a little bit so we can surge forward with even greater momentum. Always remember this: if you say nothing, you change nothing; if you change nothing, nothing will change.

Okay, so if I can make a change in a person here, that will translate to a real change over there (in the afterlife). What I would really like to know, then, is how one rids himself of old habits, old beliefs that were engrained in him since birth. I really have a hard time with this. I won't use myself as an example, because old beliefs never stuck with me to begin with when I was growing up, and perhaps one day you can explain to me why. But I have seen family members and friends who could not and would not consider any change to whatever beliefs were instilled in them since childhood. Helping others on such matters looks hard, and I would even go so far as to say impossible.

Here is a hard fact. Being resistant to changes will greatly harm your level of awareness in Dorna. Beliefs resulting from upbringing, or what we consider sentimental attachments, must be broken for progress to take shape. We will touch just a bit today on what you need to do in order to change. The problem is that most people know what is required of them, but they are either afraid or they are simply not at a place in their evolution to do the legwork.

What do you mean "people know what is required of them?"

People know right from wrong. They are great at giving advice to their fellow humans. Rightful advice. And they will acknowledge that rightful advice, but will not act upon it themselves. Not everyone who knows the path walks the path.

I know what you're saying. It's easy to give the right advice. Though I believe advice given by one who lives by his own words can serve a greater impact on the recipient.

Living the right way as discussed in the first book will elevate you to the seventh plane and perhaps even beyond.

You speak of change so we can reach a plane beyond the seventh, and you've chosen as your analogy a climber on a mountain. But even a great climber sometimes runs into problems at a level higher than any he's reached before, problems that may, at worst, end his life. With no way of coming back down to prepare for his climb again, I ask, don't you think the unknown may be an end to the soul just as death here is an end to the physical body?

Absolutely. It may be an end. For one phase of our evolution. A person on the mountain at a point beyond the known may die indeed. This death may be an end in one world, but nevertheless a beginning in another. Passing to the eighth plane may not allow us to return to Dorna or the physical dimension, but it may open a new way of existence – a third way of existence we have yet to wrap our minds around. We will, though, when we reach it.

You speak of us being born Pathians. I assume at birth we're positioned in the greatest plane available yet. But the chain reaction of our upbringing along with its connected influence to society effectively pulls us down to lower levels. Am I getting it right?

You come in to this world a Pathian. If you are to continue moving in the right direction, in the natural way God intended for us, you will definitely end up at the seventh plane. Once you are here, it is hard to move lower. It is regrettable that souls are so easily influenced and manipulated from within channels other than the seventh plane, which we will discuss soon. When people allow themselves to be blinded by the influences of the past, they remain static, while those who open their minds to the vast universe allow a new way of thinking and, as a result, do progress. Humans are arrogant in their nature. We used to be arrogant in our nature as well. It is only when we decided that we cannot allow our know-it-all egos to dictate our lives that we found we soared to higher levels. This single act has profoundly changed our lives for the better. This act of opening our minds to new ideas allowed us to reject old ways.

Since we aren't going to dwell on the particular changes needed, can you at least share a few principles that can help us in our development?

One single powerful tool. "Do *not* do unto others what you do *not* want others to do unto you." We truly would like everyone to pay attention to what this phrase teaches us and take it to the extreme. It is the most powerful tool we could ever teach you, and we truly mean it: whatever you do not like do not force on others. You hate when religion is forced on you, so do not force yours on others. You hate it when people steal from you, so do not steal from others. You like peace and quiet, so be peaceful and quiet. You hate restrictions, so do not restrict. You like to be free, so do not oppress others. And when we say this powerful tool should be enacted by *everyone*, we speak of family members like our sons and daughters as well. We know it may be extremely hard to allow your kids the same freedom you have, but this is perhaps the fastest way to propel us to the eighth plane and beyond. Such behavior implemented with the many powers at our disposal will always put us ahead of any crowd lacking in this understanding.

Such as?

Power of content.

You have indeed awakened my inner questioning power.

You are using the power of questions quite well, but allow us to reserve our explanation on the power of content for when the time is right.

Sometimes I'm not sure how we can progress when we have yet to settle the argument of creationism versus evolutionism.

You know where we stand on this one. We are definitely created by God's hand, but are nevertheless able to evolve independently from Him. Us and all that He ever seeded. We strongly hold to our opinion that we must continue to evolve, in particular, beyond the falsehood of "Biblical creationism."

Creationism became a political tool supported by many officeholders and businesses alike, ones that simply used it to further their own agendas. It baffles me how people would take a stand in support of something even though they themselves do not believe it.

Evolution remains the backbone of our spiritual continuation. And a lack of progress will remain so long as people are ignorant about the world around them. You see, most people do not even understand science – what it is or how it works. They avoid it as if it is not a part of God's creation. To adequately understand evolution, you must open your mind and think like a scientist, which is really hard for most of you, but will remain a fundamental element for our growth. You must broaden your horizon by studying in detail a vast number of disciplines like cellular biology, genetics, anatomy, geology, paleontology, chemistry and technology. Many have no clue about these areas whatsoever. Try explaining evolution to them when all they know is creationism based on a few written words inscribed thousands of years ago in one chapter of one book. They assumed this mindset with no effort and no questions. So long as it stays this way, those who believe in creationism will remain forever locked in a prison of ignorance.

I find it hard to persuade them when they lack even a basic understanding of the one thing they depend on for their knowledge – the Bible.

The ability to question is our greatest privilege as Pathians. Questioning will remain the essence of our intelligence, and we know more not because we question what we do not know, but rather we question what we *do* know.

I live by it. It's hard to continue though when most people remain living in the past. Furthermore, they fear the afterlife as a consequence to questioning or doubting their beliefs.

This is where "222" comes into play. Promote "222" as the symbol of continuity that is "the afterlife," where everything becomes right. We would also like you to adopt the symbol of infinity to this leaderless movement, as it describes the true nature of who both we and you are.

Is there an easy way to change oneself?

Always. Change is not that hard.

How?

Imagination.

What can you accomplish with imagination? Perhaps it's the greatest power you have over there, but here, imagination is just—

Never underestimate the power of imagination. Many accomplishments started with imagination. It is the single most influential power ever to exist. Whether you act on it or not, imagination can and will align your particles to higher planes, furthering your understanding of the universe. *But*, and this is a big but, for imagination to work, one must allow his mind to be free and provide it with the fuel it so sorely needs. In other words, even though imagination is freed by the mind, it remains limited due to the lack of experience on the part of the one imagining. To expand your ability to imagine, you must understand the process for which imagination is dependent. By educating yourself and exposing yourself to the endless varieties of possibilities and experiences, true or not, right or wrong, you will provide the ingredient that carries your imagination to higher ground. In short, you cannot imagine if there is nothing to base your imagination on.

Does a lack of knowledge about God prevent you from imagining God better?

It does. But the good news is that the further we ascend up the planes, the better we can imagine. And our imagination will come up with theories and assumptions that one day will become true, furthering our imagination even more.

Which means?

Remember when we said *you* are God? Well, become like God, feel like God. Now do not confuse one god with another. Do not try to become like the God of the Bible. Do not wish to be worshipped. Do not wish to cause havoc and chaos. Wish to become like the true God, an adventurer with great abilities. You must become like God through its only true meaning. "I am that I am. I am what I am." Free your mind in the only place that you can – in the passage while you are dreaming. Ponder it well. We started talking about this in our first book. Think how those two simple statements can also help in your daily life, eliminating pride and jealousy.

Enabling uniqueness.

Those phrases that describe God well require more thinking outside the box, as they not only enable uniqueness, but also align the thinker with God.

Can the force of God be attained through such a method?

We acknowledge our limitations when it comes to understanding God, and this is no different. To achieve God's abilities through imagination is something we will perhaps never grasp, but to go down that path in an effort to align ourselves with as much as we are able has already yielded many rewards.

You speak of controlling our dreams as a way to practice being more in control while we are fully in the grip of the passage, but what about when we are in the physical dimension? What about when we are not asleep?

You have got the power of meditation on your side. You must learn how to free your mind, but you must learn how to contain it as well. That is when the power of meditation comes into play. Specifically, "Awaken Meditation."

Awaken Meditation? Never heard of it.

It's the ability to be in a constant state of meditation, to allow your soul full control of your thoughts and emotions. We will speak about this in greater detail at another time. Before we move on from this subject though, we would like to give this piece of advice to anyone who wishes to practice control of their dreams while in the passage: when you get up in the middle of the night, right after you have come out of the grip of the passage, but while still remembering the dream, as tired as you may be, sit up and go into meditation. Immediately clear your mind from the dream. It is extremely difficult, but once mastered, it will provide an amazing sensation and sense of absolute control.

Why in the night, and why after a dream?

Your main sources of sensory input – namely your eyes and ears – are not being bombarded with the same onslaught of stimuli that occurs throughout the day. Though you may still hear noises coming from inside or outside of the house that you normally do not hear during the day due to all the other distractions, it is still fairly minute in comparison, allowing your mind to tune it all out rather easily. And coming out of a dream when all your senses have been overstimulated, then bringing it to a complete halt, will let you reap the benefits we mentioned before. It is like running a full mile, sweating and panting, and then instantaneously bringing your breathing and heartbeat to a normal pace. It is full control of the mind.

Your analogy is impossible. There is no way we can control the inner workings of our bodies like that.

You may not be able to control the inner workings of your body, but you can most definitely control your mind. That analogy was meant for you to *imagine* how powerful such control would feel.

What exactly is the mind? Isn't it the soul? What exactly are we trying to achieve?

We are trying to hone the soul's ability to control its actions in both the physical body and in the passage. We do not like to be beholden to our environment, as it limits control of our development.

In the first book, you used the battery as an analogy for our soul's ability to hold more energy.

We would rather describe it as a flexible, expendable fishing net. A net allows energy to flow through it. It can expand and contract and is able to hold valuables when needed. This description can also explain the soul's interaction with God's particles.

Does this phenomenon happen in the physical world?

Of course. Although it is not happening directly with God's particles, but rather as a result of his interaction with your world. In fact, it is happening right now as we speak. Information is buzzing through the air, passing you by on a regular basis. Some of the information you are able to process with your senses, and some requires proper equipment. Either way, you are always interacting with information, particles of knowledge, sound and light. With the use of an open mind and the occasional piece of equipment, you are able to trap more of what was once hidden from you.

Does this cycle ever end? Will there be a time when we can no longer observe more? Where there is no need for further interaction?

It ends when you decide it ends. And it is endless if you decide it is endless. We observe you all the time. We see a lot of people situated on the seventh plane, yet they have slowed down or altogether stopped their search for more understanding. This is how you find yourself at the top, but still stunted by all accounts. This is how a person's intelligence can become an obstacle that further obscures the purpose of our return.

Chapter 7

The Return

Now that you've explained where we're going and how we get there, it's perhaps a good time to explain how we come back here. I understand that the passage may allow you to return so long as the soul is still connected to the body, but you've also made it quite clear that once a soul passes the point of no return, there's absolutely no chance it can come back that same route. Now, reincarnation is a belief shared by many religions, but none have yet explained to my satisfaction how the soul travels back into a body. How does the process work? In the first book, you spoke of the channels as methods of return, not to mention the idea of using astrology as a map for that return. Perhaps you can provide us with just a quick recap before I bombard you with questions.

What you call astrology we call an ever-evolving map that shows us the way to the physical dimension – our practice playground. It is not a map per se, but a glowing path visible in the spirit world that, once a soul attaches itself, will guide it all the way to its earthly destination once more. Now that you are familiar with the concept of the seven planes of Dorna, it is easy to understand how channels that stream to the physical dimension from the seventh plane are not visible nor accessible to spirits from lower levels. The channels vibrate at different rates corresponding with the levels they originated from. It is why a lower level spirit cannot transcend via a channel that vibrates at higher rates.

I really don't understand the need for this sort of complexity. Why do we need this cycle at all? I understand the purpose of our return; it's just that I'd like to ask the Creator why.

That is a question we ask ourselves all the time, a question that only God can answer. As for us, we are not sure we will ever know the reason for this enigma. What we do know is that we are making the best of it, and we will never stop exhausting every opportunity to make the best of it.

How do the planes generate the channels?

The channels do not start at the planes. They originate from within your world.

But you just said the channels are connected to the corresponding levels they originated from.

Yes, they are connected. But they *originate* from within the physical dimension, crossing directly into the afterlife. They originate from a source that vibrates the same way as the planes from which they cross. They originate from a woman. She is the gate opener, one who can reach between our worlds.

Interesting.

It is, in fact, quite amazing. A woman is the key to the channels. If a woman belongs to the first plane because of her understanding, then she is able to open only the channel to the first plane. On the other hand, if a woman's understanding is of the seventh level, then she is able to open channels to all seven planes.

How can a woman open the channels? How can they bridge between Heaven and Earth?

Through the apparatus of procreation that lies in every woman. We are, of course, speaking of the female reproductive system. It is the seed, the egg. It is the channel generator.

Which I assume is influenced by the reproductive system of the male?

The female egg is what ignites the opening and flow of the channel. It is done on a regular basis during the reproductive life of the female. The channel continues to open monthly, yet it is only by male reproductive assistance that this channel holds strong.

I knew we were good for something. Humor aside though, can you explain how it is that a female who belongs to the seventh plane can establish, via the channel, a connection to all seven planes?

It would have been extremely hard to explain a few hundred years ago let alone thousands of years ago. Any change done to the physical body leaves a mark within us and on the next generation to come. It is a signature you call DNA. It is what defines you, and it is through spiritual changes that you can affect your DNA, which in turn helps affect your outcome in the next life. It is via this method that the body knows how to open the channel and connect it to the rightful plane.

Then what's the problem with reaching the eighth plane if every female who's from the seventh plane can reconnect with it and open channels that allow more souls to return?

The seventh plane seems to backfire on us. As we grow in our understanding, we tend to be more peaceful with ourselves. We grow tired of society's attitudes. We tend to dissocialize, causing us to negate the need for a family, which prevents new channels from holding strong and cuts the lifeline of our continued journey. Being on higher planes has many side effects that we must learn to master. Side effects that must be repaired. Side effects that have brought an unjustified sense of comfort and superiority. For us, this is a drawback, a poison that paralyzes our continuity. We must not be comfortable nor act superior. We must be able to discern that spirituality is not only related to understanding, but also doing.

You're going to have to explain that further at some point, but for now, can you tell me how exactly the channel opens?

When the egg is released from the ovary, the body releases (through its natural process) hormones controlled by the brain, which initiate the microscopic channel, which in turn stays connected to the egg. At this stage, the channel is as strong as it will be, and it stays that way until the demise of the egg through natural biological process unless thanks to the male sperm – the seed that seals the connection between our worlds keeps it viable, and so, does the channel.

Though the Bible is not so gracious with women, it does heavily emphasize the notion that a woman can create and simultaneously destroy. Your words seem to suggest the same. A woman can decide the fate of society – our fate from evolving beyond the seventh plane.

Women are and always will be the bridge between our worlds. Without them, we are no more. They hold our future in their hands. Whether they build us up and progress us or oversee our demise, the power is theirs.

Can a soul connect through the open channel if a male sperm does not seed the egg to hold it strong?

No, it cannot. Why are you asking?

If a channel is simply a natural event and relies on the male sperm to seed it in order to keep it open so that a soul can connect with the body, then it throws out the window the possibility of a virgin birth.

Are you about to vent?

You know me too well. I read once (not sure where) that even within the Christian faithful, there are only but a small percentage who actually believe in the virgin birth. Yet every Sunday, they lead their family to church to hear this same old story as if it were true. That the historical Jesus was born of a virgin. So, now that you speak of the channels as a natural event, I was thinking, if Jesus's birth was a miracle performed by God, one that negated the need for a male sperm, why leave an opening for doubt? Why bring forth the son of God through a natural event well known to all? Why not bring him in a manner unassociated with natural events? People forget the book of Genesis and, specifically, the creation of Adam. If the God of the Bible can create

Adam in a day, then why not send His own son Jesus in a similar fashion? Why wait nine months via a well-established natural process? Why not have the son of God appear out of thin air with special effects in front of the thousands of pilgrims at Jerusalem in the holy temple during one of the major holidays like Passover? If Jesus is God, or the son of God, then why choose a normal process for his incarnation?

Because, as we established before, Jesus is not God, but rather an elevated spirit who came back through a normal process that all spirits, regardless of their understanding, go through.

Why then call yourself the son of God (if that is what he called himself)?

Because he *is* the son of God. You are, too. So are we. All souls are.

Why tell everyone that he and God are one and the same (if that is what he said)?

Because he *is* a part of God. You are, too. So are we. All souls are.

Did the Virgin Mary get pregnant through the direct intervention of God?

No. But it was an intervention nonetheless. An intervention every soul goes through. In Jesus's case, it was the natural way his soul chose its path. That path started through a natural process initiated by a woman and maintained by the seed of a physical man. The true God – not the one represented by the Bible – has created a system of continuations that require no intervention. That is His greatness. That said, we do agree with you that it is bizarre why the God of the Bible, who created Heaven and Earth and all that lies within it in six days, ends up using a natural event to bring forth His son in order to show His power. We share your frustration.

It's good to know I'm not the only one who sees this. If only I can influence those who believe in religion to ask the right questions.

You will. Just keep on doing what we ask of you.

I still have a bit of a hard time though understanding the hardship we face in bridging the seventh plane. And how do the channels provide us with the means to progress?

It is time for a metaphor.

The mountains.

Actually, the seven-story building this time. But before we go there, we would like to explain a few things. You have originated via the seventh channel, which contains tools that help you progress with greater ease. Tools you already own. Tools such as patience, intelligence, and many others. Tools that give you a great deal to push forward with. Tools that position you at a better starting point than others. Tools you have already acquired, generated by the same people responsible for opening the channel. We are talking about your parents. Their life here and the choices they made are reflected within their DNA, which is responsible for a particular energy signature. That signature is then carried via the channel to its destined plane. Let's start with the metaphor of the building. A seven-story building will again represent Dorna's seven planes. The space outside will represent the physical dimension. On the outside, right in front of the building, stand many different types of people. They all have different strengths. Each person has the task of throwing a rope to other people situated on different planes, who in turn are trying to catch the rope so they can tie it off and climb down. However, the rope can only be used once, and then it breaks. The first person, whose energy is low, can only throw the rope to the first floor, ultimately allowing just one person to climb down. Whichever floor/plane a person originated from will reflect his ability to throw the rope. A person from a higher floor/plane will have greater strength that allows him to throw the rope to a higher level, and so on. In our scenario, as well as in reality, there are more people whose strength reach the lower levels, while only a few can reach the higher ones. This means those residing on the top floor must wait much longer for a lifeline to reach them, while those on the lower levels find themselves going up and down quite often. To complicate things a bit, not every rope is the same, just as not all people are the same. If a rope reaches the seventh floor and can only hold a hundred pounds, it automatically eliminates the possibility that heavier people can come down, further increasing the length of time it takes for a person to descend from that plane.

This is so complex.

There is more.

Okay. But why is it that the seventh plane is so hard to reach?

The seventh plane does not receive many connections – the ropes that enable us to come back – which prevents those souls from returning more often to Earth, their practice ground for gaining new abilities. Our building has more channels open on the bottom because there are more souls originating from them, while the seventh plane has but a few. Since we can traverse all planes, the urge to live life in the physical world leaves us no choice but to return via a channel lower than our abilities. It is a path lots of us do not wish to take, but it nevertheless helps in sharpening already acquired capabilities.

You mean to say that a soul on the seventh plane may choose a channel on the sixth or —

Even the first. Yes, we are saying that. Have you ever seen a child with unusual intelligence coming from a family lacking in it, or one growing up with attitudes and beliefs completely different from his background, as if he does not belong?

Yes, I have.

Though we ride a channel using tools we have already mastered, the seventh plane's teaching and experiences remain with us, putting us at odds with our family if they are not aligned with us. It is, nevertheless, good practice for us – sharpening our already acquired skills, trying ourselves to see how we would act should we find ourselves in a situation other than the one we have already mastered. Besides, it is exhilarating to experience life in the physical dimension no matter where we place ourselves.

How does the channel establish a connection with the soul in the afterlife?

For you to understand that, we need to explain a bit more about the channels. Each channel is unique, much like a DNA pattern; there is no other like it. Each carries an energy signature supplied by the male and female who were responsible for originating the channel. To explain it better, let's use a five-digit number as an analogy. In our case, since we are talking about the seventh plane, each channel generated via a seventh plane originator shall have "7" as the first digit. This first number is the signature that enables the channel to vibrate higher and penetrate the seventh plane of Dorna. The rest of the digits will represent the change and experience gathered by the higher of the two originators. So, if the female is on a higher plane than the male, her signature will be more dominant, and vice versa. The rest of the digits may appear as "7-4256," with the numbers after the seven representing the position of the channel as it connects to the afterlife. While this example has only five digits in order to simplify your understanding, the truth is that a channel's signature contains *millions* of digits. To us, the connection, the identification, and the decision that follows thereafter comes as second nature. We could go on and on, speaking of this process for days, but believe us when we say that the more we speak of the connection, the more confusing it would be. Just know this: the more people change, the more we can fill the seventh channel, and the easier it will be to bridge the seventh plane.

And the planning of the return? You've said you plan your return. Doesn't sound very "natural" to me.

We have found that when we intervene in the natural event of a connection, the faster that event takes place. And since we are all family here, we plan and take turns so we can advance higher faster. This is perhaps a bit more complex, but our return to your world is planned meticulously so that every move and effort will result in greater advancement toward our destiny of breaching the seventh plane and in greater preparedness of our continuation thereafter.

You're intervening with natural events.

What is natural? Aren't we a part of nature? Aren't you? In the physical world, you have modified animals, plants and topography in every direction. You intervene in a natural way. But what is the natural way? Doesn't a creator intervene in a natural way as well? You, us – we are creators. And as long as that act is applied in a sensible way, it is a natural way. It follows who we are in the scheme of God.

You've mentioned this planning before. How you come together and plan the return of a soul, standing by his side to support him. But I'll be honest, it's a bit weird for me to think that coming back can be planned by mere souls inhabiting a spirit's body.

As weird as two people who come together and decide to have offspring? As weird as standing by their offspring for the better part of their lives to guide them as they develop? The physical dimension and the spiritual dimension behave in quite the same way. Which one would you say is weirder?

And the connection you make to the channel, gliding toward a newborn, reincarnated—

Is that weirder than a man and a woman connecting? Is that any weirder than the process by which a male sperm fertilizes a female egg? How would you have us connect with a newborn if not through the channels we have described when the spirit lacks any organ similar to the one that creates the connection to begin with?

That's the problem. My understanding of how things work is limited to this world. So even with imagination, it's a bit hard to comprehend. That said, I do like the notion that even when the connection is perfect for a soul to grab on to, it's still free to make a choice whether to connect or not.

Free will; everything remains our choice.

Since fertility is responsible for the creation of the channel, am I to assume that if no soul connects on the other end, that means the woman on this end is therefore unable to carry a full-term pregnancy?

Yes. The lack of acceptance by a soul to connect to the channel will cause it to close within the first few week, thereby creating what you call a "miscarriage." A soul must connect to the channel within its first week, which to us may be a matter of mere seconds. But there is, of course, another more inevitable cause: there is no one on the other end who is able to connect, no one *suitable* to connect. The result of the channel's high vibrations leads to the incapability of any soul to match it and therefore connect to it, meaning they are not yet sufficiently developed to make that connection, leaving the person in the physical dimension in a grim situation. They must try repeatedly until a soul capable of connecting has arrived from the physical dimension or a soul arrives that is finally willing to make the connection. This phenomenon is exclusively reserved to the upper planes. The lack of suitable recipients at each plane will translate in your world to a case of infertility.

This chapter is becoming so detailed, I'm afraid we'll lose our reader's interest.

We warned you about this when we started.

Yes, you did. Speak to me about the channel. How does it actually work? Does it function like the tunnel in the passage?

The channel is made out of unique positive and negative particles that reverse themselves as they interact with our worlds, allowing them to exist and flow without losing strength.

What do you mean?

The particles the channel is made of are positive on your side, but flip to negative when they pass into our dimension. It is through these particles' behavior that the channel can bridge and connect between the two dimensions.

Is that how the soul is able to bridge between the two dimensions? Does the soul flip its molecules as well?

No. The soul was and always will be made of an opposite material to your physical dimension. This is why it must remain in the passage, why it must control the physical body from afar. Our particles and yours are in complete opposition and would obliterate one another if they ever came together. We believe we are incapable of experiencing this phenomenon, nor would we like to. Knowledge such as this belongs solely to God. It is knowledge way beyond anyone's understanding.

What I'd really like to know is the physical effects of being at a higher level. What happens to the spirit?

As we are able to contain more knowledge, not through the resizing of our body's surface, but through our ability to vibrate at higher rates of speed, we interact more with God's particles that are passing by us and we then become lighter. Not lighter in a sense of weight, but lighter because we are able to defy the very thing that holds us within a plane. It is an ability that grants us an extra way of seeing the world around us. What is amazing about this is it allows us to see more of this world, and it is through this interaction that we know the views continue, as we have yet to touch the surface of this phenomenon. This is God's gift to us. A multitude of universes and a multitude of playgrounds.

That is our game plan? The eighth plane and beyond? A playground?

What else would it be? Why can't it be fun? After all, knowledge to a Pathian is nothing but pleasure. And since the multitude of universes contains so much information, one can only have more fun.

You must admit that understanding knowledge may be frustrating at times.

The good thing is that the more particles your "bucket" interacts with, the easier it is to understand. That is why the higher you are on the planes, the easier it is for you to understand, making you less resistant to new understandings. Remember, we are at the infancy of our realities. Can you even imagine how many connections we can have and where it will take us?

Why don't we remember the afterlife? I understand the well-constructed universe by God as explained in the first book that allows us to live again and again, free from the constraints of past memories, but how is it done? What mechanism enables us to forget? And why do some of us actually remember, at least at an early age?

Your memories are made of particles that cannot make the journey with you via the channels. It is the nature of the channels to strip you of your connection with Dorna. Your memories are stored in a way that is unfamiliar to you, one that does not require a solid structure. As for little children who can recall some glimpses into their past lives, it only happens when the transition from death to rebirth is fast, meaning instantaneously in our terms. You see, it takes time for the soul's memories to be fully purged in Dorna, and when you catch a channel back to the physical dimension faster than the purging process can complete, it leaves the soul with some of its memories. These memories will eventually be suppressed, but it does leave traces of them in the mind of a child, which as far as he is concerned remain a part of his life to be recalled.

Sounds like formatting a hard drive and not fully finishing.

You could probably use that analogy.

It would have been amazing to remember past lives, to remember Dorna.

You will. But trust us when we say that you do not want to remember everything while you are holding on to an earthly body and its emotions. Also, there are many among you who do not learn from past actions, let alone will they be able to learn from past lives. It is especially for them that our Creator made it this way. Making it new every time.

Okay, then if so, why keep the memories at all?

Because it serves us better here. Stripped from earthly influences, we are able to handle all memories. For us, there are no good or bad memories; just memories to interact with while we create here in Dorna.

How does it look to ride a channel into a newborn?

We call it "bonea." It is an ancient term for when the soul is in possession of a physical body. We know of the channels from what we can see and our past experiences, but we do not recall the ride. We only remember the attachment of the channel to the soul and to the physical body. There is still a sense of adventure, a sense of emerging fear, as always, of the unknown... even when it is by our own planning.

Why exactly can't you recall the ride on the channels?

The channels are made of reversing particles – positive and negative – and they do not allow memory to transfer from within. Therefore, we cannot hold on to nor connect to any memory created within the period when the soul descends toward the physical dimension. Only when we enter the physical body is our ability to remember restored, but our memory is emptied of anything made before the connection.

Why do you think the channels are like that?

Some of God's creation is meant to be hidden from us. We cannot claim to know it all, but we theorize that because part of the channel is made out of opposing particles, any memory created within the channel is annihilated on contact once the connection reverses.

Can you enter any physical body you want since your view is so wide and seems to include all planes?

Any channel within our view is within reach, only it is not limited to the physical body of a human being. We can also use animal bodies, as they are much more abundant than humans. But we prefer human form because we have progressed humanity in such a way that we can experience far more emotions than any other animal. However, to be honest, it is sometimes necessary to experience life through the differing point of view of an animal.

Like what animal?

A dog.

What can I master by being a dog?

Unconditional love. Faithfulness. Fear. Dogs are more attuned to these emotions than their human counterparts are. There are many reasons to experience a dog's life. In fact, to never have had a dog's life as a memory is to miss out on the best thing life has to offer.

Did I ever experience animal lives?

To be a Pathian means we try it all. You are a Pathian.

I'll take that as a yes. Now, if you're on the seventh plane, limited in the channels you have to choose from, and therefore decide to come back using a channel that originated from a lower plane, what does it do to you here?

You never lose what you have gained. Your memories, your experiences, and the tools you acquired are yours to keep. In other words, choosing one channel from one plane over another will not rob you of the ground you made in Dorna. It is why people with great understanding find they do not belong with the family they are growing up with. It is like a rollercoaster, only it does not lose momentum going down due to friction and will bounce back up to the same level.

Do we have to come back to the physical world?

If you wish your evolution to stagnate, then you do not have to come back. Not all spirits are made equal. Some would like things to stay the way they are, so they distance themselves from the basic desire to evolve, and therefore return less frequently. Some may come back for the sake of adventure. It is, after all, a great adventure to be reborn again and again, living life as a new person each time and generating new memories. Some wait for the right channel to open up. They do not wish to miss an opportunity should they choose a path that was not originally meant for them.

Prior to this life, when was the last time I lived in a physical body?

You waited 3,300 years for the right channel to open.

That long?

It may look long in your world, but it is a much shorter period to us (albeit still a long time in incarnation terms here). Nevertheless, it is the virtue of a Pathian to be patient.

You've made it quite clear that you're not going to tell me who I was in a previous life, and I understand it has no bearing on my progress here or in the afterlife, but it would be intriguing to know whether I had, perhaps, a position of great influence in that past life. Then again, what I was before is not so important as who I am today. It's funny, when I speak to people about past lives, everyone thinks they were someone important, like a king or a queen.

There were not many kings or queens for us to have lived our lives through. And even if it is true, that you were a king or a queen, it is not important for your progress. Though past lives have great influence on who you are today as a result of all the tools you acquired, to say that a king's tools are better than a carpenter's because they look grander or more important is not true, nor do they have a greater influence on who you are in this current life.

If I could once again live in a physical body 3,300 years ago, I would choose to live in Egypt. After all, I admire the culture of the ancient Egyptians.

You never know. Actually, you will know. In time.

You say we are all born Pathians. How can I tell it so?

Being a Pathian is the natural way. Children are, by God's natural design, intentionally inquisitive. Suppress this, and you suppress their ability to evolve the Pathian way. If you take any child, no matter which channel they have come through, and position them in the hands of those connected to higher planes, you will see evolution taking place in a natural way. You see, most souls are suppressors, unable to allow ideas to process in the mind of born Pathians. If every person in the world would just grant the gift that was granted to them – the freedom to think, the freedom to extricate themselves from their elders' beliefs – then a miraculous thing would happen. We would advance as nature meant for us to.

And there'd be no need for this book. We'd be completely free to evolve. I'll never say never, but in this day and age, I think it's an impossibility.

Unfortunately, you are correct. Nevertheless, there is always the hope that one or two kids, even growing up in such a limiting environment, will keep their inquisitive spark and rediscover the power of asking – a tool granted to them by God so that when they are free from the constraints of their upbringing, they can find their way once more.

So, kids are Pathians. Perhaps I'm just as guilty as they are when it comes to questioning, although sometimes even I don't answer my son's questions. To my defense, my son asks hundreds of questions a day, and I usually end up telling him to give it a rest. The good thing – no, the amazing *thing – is that we live in an age where knowledge couldn't be more easily obtained. A flick of the finger, and you have multiple answers to one question. However, I'm not sure if we're at a better time to promote our agenda just because vast amounts of information are at our fingertips. Much of the information out there is simply false, and people fall into old patterns of believing something because "it is written." Furthermore, the art of searching eludes many. How would one bring himself to think more freely?*

You must look into the root cause of your state, meaning why are you religious? Why are you afraid? Why are you *anything* for that matter? Can you remember who you were before the world told you who you are?

How would you have done it? What would you have done to elevate your children through the channels?

We would have allowed them the freedom of belief. We would have given them a variety of information to help them discern for themselves the meaning of all beliefs available to humankind, including this one. And of course, at the right age, we would have insisted that they move out of our home.

You would have sent your own children out of your house. Why?

Because it is the most gracious thing to do. To allow your children to become who *they* need to become and not who *we* have become. Look at all nations whose culture dictates that children must move on when they are adults, and contrast it with nations whose children remain at home, even after adulthood. Any family who keeps their sons and daughters at close bay after they mature will ensure that those children are unable to develop beyond their immediate environment. It has always been true.

I want to go back to the channels themselves. You've said they're connected to astrology, the map of our return. Would you like to elaborate? How did the ancients come to learn of this?

Through the power of observation.

Observation of astrology? You mentioned in the first book that we got it wrong. I'm assuming astrology as a theory is right, yet something in our interpretation was wrong. Is that what you mean?

Associating astrology with the date you are born is wrong. Astrology relies on your birthdate to interpret who you are and what lies ahead of you. That is wrong.

Is that why certain people can't relate themselves to what astrology says they should be?

Yes.

Then to what ends should we associate astrology?

It should be associated with the date of the opening of the channel – the day that the channel held strong, from when a sperm penetrated the egg. Now, take that date and combine it with the origins of the connection (meaning where the man's and woman's planes are connected to), and you will have the most accurate ability to calculate the true path that lies ahead of the oncoming soul within a new born.

Astrology will have to be rewritten.

Astrology will have to realign. And when it is interpreted together with the originators of the channel, it will then be possible to predict with certainty the individually designated road and tools he has in his possession.

Not that this is connected to what we're talking about, but I think I understand why the Kabbalah's claim about a soul entering a rock is implausible.

Yes, it is. The soul, in order to move between worlds, must have a catalyst that triggers the disconnection and reconnection. The process of the dying brain opens the portal between our worlds.

So even though a plant may find its demise eventually, a rock doesn't have a natural trigger that ends its existence and opens up the portal.

Furthermore, even if you suggest that a rock somehow disintegrates, a variety of reasons still remain as to why it cannot serve any purpose in correcting our ways. It is only through repeated practice under the same conditions that changes can be made. Silently, being stuck in a solid state away from pretty much everything is not beneficial to us.

Based on what you've told me, I have to bring up a few more things about the Kabbalah's messages. The first is that the true nature of a newborn child is based on the thoughts that a man and woman have at the moment of conception. I read in a book that if a couple during intercourse show feelings of self-satisfaction, then the child will be born selfish and greedy; if it was conceived during intercourse with mutual understanding and love, then the child will reflect that because that's what it was given at the time of creation. Furthermore, if, say, a child is born out of rape, it will grow to be angry and violent. I always rejected this belief, as it didn't sit straight with my experience and the world I've seen around me. When I was about 15 years old, my parents decided they wanted to become foster parents. So, that same year, we adopted a few months-old baby born to a drug-addicted woman who also sold her body for a living. This baby was conceived out of a selfish desire to maintain a filthy habit, with no consideration of the consequences. If the Kabbalah teaching was correct, that little baby should've turned into a selfish, greedy, violent, self-destructive criminal. But instead, from the time this child could express herself, none of the traits the Kabbalah speaks of were visible. In fact, quite the contrary – all we saw was an amazing child who in all respects was kind, wise and loving.

All traits that you can only get through your destined channel. Traits that will accompany you your entire life. Traits that no one, no matter what, can take away from you.

I have a lot more Kabbalah teachings to vent about, but a book about the afterlife is definitely not the place.

Something tells us you will find the time at some point in the near future.

You know me all too well. Out of curiosity, why now? Why have these conversations at this point in time?

Because we are worried.

Worried? About what?

Worried that this is perhaps one of the last few times we will have to speak to you all.

What do you mean?

What happens when we get to the eighth plane? Are we still able to come back? Do we still need the benefits of reincarnation? Is it a one-way path to a new form of existence?

What if it's bad?

It simply cannot be.

Why?

Because all good things require hard work. And good follows good. It is an intuition all of us here share. There is also a noticeable pattern: birth, life, death, passage, Dorna, one of the seven planes, and back to rebirth through the channels. The pattern can change, but it shows that it moves in the right direction.

Not here it doesn't.

But it does. It is the way God's energy flows, unable to be trapped within a predestined cycle because we exercise the very thing He granted us. Freedom to inquire. Of course, this fearful view remains the primary argument for all lower levels – that the unknown is a realm of punishment for those who venture beyond the safe place. Only if we are not to return would we never know any of it, allowing them to keep on furthering their agenda.

Do you think there is a second stage of passing with its own planes and channels?

It most certainly could be. We do not know what awaits us. Whether it is a form of existence beyond what is familiar to us or whether it will happen on the eight or the ninth or the tenth plane, and so on. Regardless, we are bound to continue.

You mentioned that all children are born Pathians, including those born to parents who are connected to lower planes. Is it possible for such a child to make a jump through several planes in one lifetime?

Absolutely. Take a child raised in one country, move him to another country, disconnect him from all that he knew, and show him something new. You will be able to influence him so much, that in a matter of a few years, only but remnants of his past will remain, if anything. The height of his advancement in a situation such as this depends only partly on the channel he descended from.

Like an accent?

Accents, habits, beliefs. When we start fresh at a new place other than the one that was intended, it becomes a step forward. If it is void of influence, it is a few steps forward. Children are able to use the Pathian way to make changes very fast, but it is usually the adults who restrict them with their old-fashioned beliefs. We believe that a scientific understanding of the universe with its almost magical phenomena – galaxies, stars, and other elements that have yet to be discovered – will raise much difficulty for orthodox believers who cannot align such things with their faith. These contradictions will further harden their ability to reconcile scientific concepts with their divine books. Finally, there will be a time when the truth can no longer be suppressed and even adults will be able to leap across planes.

You think there'll be a time when we no longer need to bother improving others during our search to better ourselves? That their influence won't affect us?

One day, it may no longer be part of our agenda to have more join us.

Sounds selfish.

Not out of selfishness. We simply may not be able to. The eighth plane may be a game-changer. Perhaps, under those new conditions, we will find ourselves unable to communicate or help for reasons that are currently beyond us. The physical dimension and Dorna have completely opposite properties. We may find ourselves in a new state of existence interacting with particles we are unfamiliar with and governed by a completely new set of natural and absolute laws. Can we come back? Can we communicate? Are we still connected to this cycle of existence we are so familiar with? Maybe the new state of existence is so radical that no spirits in Dorna or the physical dimension would be able to make sense of us.

Why do you think this could happen?

Through our advancement, we continually align ourselves with God. If He talks to us through means other than His natural and absolute laws, we cannot hear Him or make sense of His message. Now, we know we are not going to be any closer to who God is – not with this understanding – but at some point on the way up, what we discuss may happen. We do not know, but we entertain this possibility. It is who we are. Besides, even if at some point we will not be able to guide, the current cycle will continue. Others will recognize the benefits of adhering to the natural and absolute laws of God, of becoming leaders, and perhaps it will be their conversations that someone like yourself will hear one day.

The eighth plane sounds a lot like "nirvana" as described by Buddhism. A freedom from the endless cycle of personal reincarnation. A place characterized by freedom from the pain and worry of the physical dimension.

It may sound similar, but it is not. While Dorna, in essence, is devoid of things like worries and pain as you are familiar with them, what we are looking for is much more than that. We are looking for understanding and abilities beyond our comprehension.

Perhaps we're meant to be leaders and to discover all of this alone. Any advice on how to become a leader? How to become a Pathian?

Every one of us has something deep down holding us back from progress. This internal hindrance is something you must identify for yourself. Find what it is and beat it down. Face your fear. Because if you do not, you are going to become just like the rest of the masses, blindly following. If, on the other hand, you choose to be unique and blaze your own trail, then rise and move forward. It is perhaps the hardest thing you will ever do, but your whole future will change. Once it is done, once you have beaten your fear, the doors of the whole universe will open before you. This is advice taken only by a few throughout the history of time. A few who have become spiritual leaders.

Chapter **8**

Earth Heaven Connection

I now understand why our dreams are so wild and crazy. I always thought that it was purely the result of our own imaginations. I suppose it is in a way, but at the same time, dreams are still manipulated by the environment of the passage; it takes over where and how our thoughts are projected. I must say it's quite a journey through sleepy time, and there are moments when I become anxious to see what awaits me that night. Most of my dreams are worthy of an Oscar, but I doubt any movie director would be interested in a series of chaotic, absurd and chronologically inaccurate events.

It is of great interest to us. In your world, you are defined by rules based on logic. Only dreams adhere to rules we have yet to discover, and it fascinates us. We know it is the key to our future.

What do you mean?

In Dorna as well as the physical world, energy will follow the natural and absolute laws of God. It is predictable and unbreakable. Yet in the passage where dreams are made, energy is never at the same intensity nor does it flow in a consistent direction. If it follows a pattern or set of laws, we have yet to decipher it. As such, we must determine that the passage does not follow any rules (unless we conclude that a chaotic, nonrepeating pattern is a rule in and of itself.)

I see.

Dreams may seem weird and eschew rules, yet we find them quite normal, beneficial and even essential to our development. It is and will remain our training ground. Furthermore, the passage remains the gateway to understanding the inner workings of God's mind.

Will we ever?

Never say never. That is a phrase we adhere to. Perhaps a glimpse into the workings of God's mind shall be sufficient enough to quench our thirst in our quest to understand God.

Why do you think we have this thirst?

We are created through the power of God, inheriting His traits, and unlike others, we choose to nourish it. Therefore, to understand God, we must understand who we are and our purpose in this world (as well as beyond).

Why do we have nightmares? Is it the product of our own doing, or do you have a helping hand in it?

What constitutes a "nightmare?" Is it what you are afraid of? Is it good? Is it bad? To us, it is none. The principles of controlling your dreams relate to good and bad dreams alike. Sometimes they occur when our worlds mingle. Sometimes we manipulate your dreams in order to advance your ability to overcome weaknesses. But on most occasions, it is merely a product of your own thoughts manifested inside the passage, in a place that has no rules, taking a dream in an unforeseeable direction. Your ability to control your emotions, and in particular the direction of the dream, continues to greatly reveal your development within Dorna.

How can I control the outcome of a nightmarish dream?

Sometimes the control is not within your dream. Sometimes the control is when you wake up.

How?

First, waking yourself up is one way to control a reality that has no physical effect on you. Second, how do your emotions react? Are you still scared after you realize it was just a dream?

So, waking up is our way of control? In a way, it's like a mind game.

Kind of. A game with benefits.

And causing our nightmares is part of your need to advance us? You're turning everything upside down. You're making bad look good.

It is what it is. When we intervene, it is based on an agreement we had with you prior to your departure from Dorna. Most nightmares are not of our doing. But when we do intervene, we give you nightmares so you may practice, so you may defeat fears and other traits you are here to overcome.

Why do it? Why use evil for teaching?

Assume you lived among only good people and were able to ignore the fact that evil existed, not acknowledging or preparing for it because it was out of sight. When evil eventually did surface, you would not have the tools to deal with it. So, the day you master your ability to control dreams – including nightmares and their effects – will be the day you master fear. Not a particular fear, but rather all fear. You see, fear has such a strong hold on us that when it surfaces, it has a tendency to interfere with our emotions and ability to make right choices.

Do you watch us all the time?

We take great interest in our future. And though you and many others remain contributors to our development, which requires our attention, our body remains busy in the daily task of living in Dorna, inhibiting our ability to constantly watch over you. Moreover, the effort to open a link between us gets harder and harder the further we go up the advancement ladder, making this task more complex and limiting it to short bursts of viewing.

It would be easier if you were on lower planes.

True.

Then why distance yourself from the Earth / Heaven connection?

Because we are Pathians. We follow in the footsteps of God. There is nothing within the natural and absolute laws of God that require us to have these conversations. In fact, it is by His laws that we are required to move on, even at the risk of distancing ourselves or, worse, completely disconnecting.

How is it that you came to that realization?

Because we have seen it again and again. Anytime, anywhere, including in our world, whenever you distance yourself from where you started, you gain an enormous amount of knowledge. And in every case, you increase your advantage over those who have remained behind, even as your ability to communicate becomes more of a challenge. Only great things happen when you acquire new knowledge and are able to see more of what exists.

The world may have acted that way before, but today, we have the internet and telephone, which have opened up our ability to access information and instantaneously connect to one another, even at great distances. Why can't it be the same?

That is true, technology has brought the world closer together. But while information is accessible, the world remains distant. And though communication is instantaneous, many still lack the tools to communicate. In addition, the fact remains that even with all this technological advancement, only those who venture away from the place of their upbringing will advance. Now, if we were to compare technological advancement with our inability to communicate easily, it would be as if we were stationed on a distant star. Our ability to speak weakens the further away we are.

You speak of leaving families behind and moving far away to spark our advancement, but it is really hard. I know it firsthand.

In this day and age, with your ability to obtain information through the internet, it is no longer necessary to physically leave the place of your upbringing; but it is nevertheless important to leave old faith behind in order to acquire new knowledge. We shall speak of this in greater detail in our next book, but just to be clear, we do not necessarily mean that you abandon your family and move on to another place all by yourself. You can seek knowledge in the place of your upbringing, but the change is harder, as you are prone to constant criticism from those who have not opened their minds to new thoughts.

What if the whole family moved to a new place?

Great advancement can happen to that family as a whole if they simply let it. But more commonly, a family who raises you in constraints will remain constrained, even upon arriving at a new destination. We know it is harsh to the ears, but it is the truth as we see it. Family, friends and culture will remain the single largest stranglehold on human development, which adversely affects us all.

And should the eighth plane wind up being the ticket out of the Earth / Heaven connection, thereby resulting in no more communications, would that be acceptable?

In our effort to advance and understand God, yes, that is acceptable.

I have a question I've wanted to ask you for a long time. Not a question of great spiritual importance, but a personal question that I'm sure has gone through the mind of many who felt your existence when you do watch us. What about our private moments when we want no prying eyes? And I speak about all we do that constitutes our private time.

We do not have emotions; therefore, we do not judge nor have any opinion (good or bad) about what you do during your private moments, nor does your doing have any effect on your spirit body in Dorna so long as you are not in violation of the natural and absolute laws of God.

But have you thought during those times to maybe close the connection and allow us the decency of our privacy?

Every observable moment, regardless of the situation, is one cherished by us, and as you will see, will also be cherished by you when the time has come. What you do in your private time (in particular what you may consider the *most* private) we will not mention here, but we will say that what you think of as "bad" all people do regardless of the plane they occupy. It is part of learning and understanding how to rid yourself of that which is considered wrong by society, and to accept the truth that your behavior is nothing other than normal behavior. If we are speaking of private sexual moments specifically, there is nothing wrong with it, but know that the mind has developed faster than the body, and the rate of sexual desire is an old remnant that the developing body has yet to catch up with.

I can only imagine how advanced one can get in Dorna once one masters imagination in the passage.

You have no idea. Mastering imagination is the engine of our continuation.

Perhaps it's not the best time to speak about what scientists say causes dreams, but I will say it bewilders me why society in general refuses to acknowledge how reasoning with no proof remains just a theory. To say that our brain is solely responsible for all that we spoke of is a refusal to acknowledge that there could be a mechanism beyond our ability to foresee.

It will remain this way so long as imagination is not used to its full potential. Outside activities beyond your world control the brain cycles as they are measured and will remain elusive so long as scientists think within the boundaries of the known world. Sleep paralysis, hypnic jerks, exploding head syndrome, and the like are all results of the soul's control and grip on the brain rather than a function of the brain alone.

I've experienced it all. What's your explanation for the exploding head syndrome? It's so freaky. You wake up because you've heard a really loud noise, sometimes combined with a flash of light.

The explosion you hear is the soul connecting to or disconnecting from the mind.

What is your location in time and space?

We are everywhere.

I want to know your exact location.

Our location in relation to you is fluid and shifts direction all the time. We exist in relation to your observations. We understand it is hard for you to conceive of a fluid, unfixed location, but Dorna is just that. In the simplest terms, the direction in which you observe is where we are.

If I look to the right, you're there, and if I look to the left, you're there just as well?

Yes.

That's so bizarre. I've never heard of anything in nature that behaves this way. However, I understand that your world operates under different laws.

It is recognized by PIER scientists that different dimensions of existence may operate under different sets of rules. And they do. However, they still fall into what we call the natural and absolute laws of God, which include the various dimensions in our visible and invisible light spectrum.

That would include the eighth plane.

Time will tell what other laws await us.

I'd like to speak about miracles. After all, I believe a miracle would constitute the greatest link between Heaven and Earth. I've read of many miracles that supposedly happened in my lifetime as well as in ancient times, but recently, because of my connection to Israel, I was told of a particular miracle pertaining to the 2014 Israel-Gaza conflict. The Iron Dome, a mobile air defense system, was unable to intercept a rocket launched from Gaza. *The rocket was heading toward a major facility in Tel Aviv only to be deflected in the final moments before impact by a sharp gust of wind, sending it into the Mediterranean Sea. Many called it a miracle from God. Could it be God?*

No. God does not generate miracles in this way. This is pure chance.

Could it be you? I mean spirits alike?

We doubt it. We have never seen any spirits move objects in such ways. This event, if true, is merely the result of a natural phenomenon.

Why can't spirits move objects?

We are great at many things, and yes, we can even move small objects. But a large object let alone a rocket in motion is beyond us. Our abilities remain strong with manipulating minds.

Why then can't it be God?

Because if God caused that miracle, why that particular rocket and not all the thousands of other rockets that were launched? Why not make a miracle to save all those who have perished on both sides of the conflict, Palestinian and Israeli? They are, after all, indistinguishable in the eyes of God. The fact is there was no miracle. You just choose to celebrate that one action, which turns out to be nothing more than a statistical probability, while simultaneously choosing to ignore all the other rockets that did get through.

I agree with you on this matter. I cannot understand how one would dismiss all other facts in order to conclude that this one possible result was a miracle. You've explained that God does not intervene in our affairs. A miracle would be where both sides wake up one day, their hearts soften, and they realize they are no different. They realize that both can live peacefully with one another, perhaps even with no borders, under one shared state. I assume God does not make miracles.

Earth / Heaven Connection

We did not say that. We did not say God does not make miracles.

Then what did you mean?

We have never witnessed any miracle by God, but that does not mean He does not perform any.

You'd better explain that. I'm getting confused now. Does God make or does He not make miracles?

We are not sure ourselves. We believe God's miracles are simply not observable. Let's take the 9/11 attack on the United States as an example. We know for a fact it happened. But what if God made a miracle, and the towers never fell because the terrorists never attacked because God had change their hearts, therefore changing the future as we know it? We would not even be able to recognize the miracle because the event would never have happened in the first place.

Then how would I know? How would I be able to recognize a miracle if I'm not even aware an event that was supposed to take place did not take place?

Therein lies the need for our progress. One day, as we grow in our understanding of the mind and ways of God, we will perhaps be able to recognize when those miracles happen. Perhaps we will be able to recognize the shift in events. We will be able to discern it was God's intervention. Until then, neither us nor you are able to discern a true miracle by God, but can only observe events resulting from natural phenomenon interpreted at our own discretion.

So, miracles—

Listen, you cannot call a low percentage of good things that happen as a consequence of a bad or misfortunate event a miracle. You have to familiarize yourself with the way the world works. Give a little more credit to God's abilities. He does not concern Himself with minor diffusions of bigger events.

In the previous book, you mentioned you have the capability to manipulate us, to manipulate the direction of our thoughts. In fact, you mentioned how easy it is for us to be manipulated by you. You probably already know where I'm going with this. Can you manipulate us in such a way that we'd believe we'd witnessed a miracle? And how grand are your abilities? Are they directed at one person or can they be directed at many simultaneously? Can you see what I'm getting it? If our minds are so fragile and prone to manipulation, how many miracles that have ever happened are simply figments of our own imaginations?

We are capable of said manipulation, but it requires a bit more elaboration. Our power is stronger when you are asleep, but is nevertheless accessible when you are awake as well. Many years ago, we became aware that subtle nudges of manipulation in awakened stages had more effect on the soul than when it was asleep. For this single reason, the body while awake cannot disassociate itself from the fact that what it sees may be a manipulation of the senses, and will therefore accept it as truth, even when it is in defiance of God's known laws. Manipulation through dreams can also serve the same purpose, although it is always associated with a fantasy that is easily dismissible. The simple answer to your questions is yes, we are able to influence your mind through infusion of supernatural thoughts within your reality.

I'll get back to the "miracles" question shortly, but if you're so advanced, then why not just manipulate your way into the minds of the people and guide them to our cause?

The higher you are in your evolution, the further away you are from your connection with the physical plane, thereby diminishing your ability to influence in such ways. Nor would we want to even if we could, as we believe the only way for one to advance is to make a change through self-awareness.

Are you telling me that advancement not only robbed us from the much-needed influence of Dorna, but it has given a permanent edge to those who reside in the lower planes to continue their strong influence on those we so need to attract?

Unfortunately, yes. But again, we do not attract; we *enlighten*. We do not persuade of our cause; we give sufficient reasoning to question.

I would like to go back to my previous questions regarding miracles, only this time I would like to redirect you to other phenomena that we don't classify as miracles – ones that are observed by many and nevertheless go unobserved by many. I'm referring to unexplained phenomena like UFO's, crop circles, fire balls and shadow people. Some such events I've witnessed personally. What can you share about that?

A lot. But it is not a story for this time. Perhaps the only phenomenon relevant to Dorna that we can discuss are the entities that you call "shadow people."

I've received many questions regarding the shadow people. Witnesses describe catching a shadowy figure out of the corner of their eye, but when they'd look directly, it would disappear. Only moments later would it reappear again in the corner of their eye. Some claim they could see them head on. I want to know what they are. Our imagination, ghosts, other spiritual entities, demons, time travelers, aliens, perhaps interdimensional beings?

They are Earthbound spirits, or ghosts if you prefer. They have traversed the passage for so long, they have lost their identity. A lost soul can only project what it knows. Spending an extended length of time in a chaotic place can strip away the awareness of identity, restricting the soul to project its image in its simplest form: a shadow.

Why can some only see them through the corner of their eye while others can see them straight on?

All Earthbound souls, including those you see in the form of shadow people, project themselves not only as a materialized apparition, but also by connecting to your line to Dorna. Some have called it the "third eye," or the mystical seeing "all eye," but it is not. It is simply you tapping into your line of existence so that they can bring themselves into your awareness. You see them in the corner of your eye because you find yourself subconsciously in tune with your soul, which nevertheless shares the same space within which Earthbound souls navigate. It is in the moment when you shift your eyes that you tune yourself out of your line and away from being able to see them anymore.

But they are still there.

They are. Earthbound spirits are always around you.

And those who can see them straight on or for longer periods of time?

Are more in tune with their line.

Hmmm. I'm not sure everyone would like to be in tune enough to see them. Are shadow people bad? Are they evil? Through my research, I've not found any indication they've caused any harm other than to maybe frighten a few.

They are not bad or evil; just lost. They have been in the passage longer than they should, and they should be redirected toward home.

What do you mean?

Point them to the light. Any light.

Seriously, point to a light? Sure, why not just tell them the minute after we gain our composure? You know, right after being scared to death! That fear is what some believe draws them to us to begin with. They hunger for fear.

They are harmless. They may scare you, but it is not their intention. The reason we ask you to point and not speak is because, at this stage, they are unable to communicate. However, redirecting their attention to a light (any light) will make more impact since they are susceptible to suggestions that they can make sense of. By encouraging them to move toward the light, it will eventually lead them back to us and to who they once were.

Let's speak more about ghosts. I myself have seen them plenty of times, as we've already discussed. Ghosts that we see are spirits who have decided not to go into the afterlife, but rather chose to stay within the passage because, for some reason, their connection to the physical world couldn't be severed. I've learned that they cannot harm us, but they most definitely will unintentionally scare us. Those like myself who were not prepared for them feared them at the beginning, but as I learned the reasons for their behavior, I relaxed and figured out how to ignore them over time. That said, why can't everyone see ghosts?

Everyone *can* see ghosts, but not everyone *will* see them. We know it does not make sense, but bear with us. The eye is just an instrument that detects light. The brain is what tells you what you see. We are either born with the ability to decipher information perceived by the eye, or we develop this ability through mental training. It is the same with drawing. Some are born with the gift, while others will study and practice, and yet others, no matter how hard they try, will never achieve a level of artistic ability beyond drawing simple stick figures – at least not in this lifetime. The brain is just the same. You either have the talent bestowed on you as a gift through God's creation, or you develop it through practice in this lifetime and the ones before in order to achieve the same ability.

How does it work?

The brain removes the image for which it has no ability to process. That is why you can have multiple witnesses watching while only a few can see.

If most are unable to see ghosts, which are in fact souls trapped in a dimension that's closer to us than Dorna, how can one even come close to feeling the presence of spirits who are two dimensions away? I speak of mediums and psychics, of course.

Through the connection of your own line. We have told you all humans are connected to their spirits via a link or line of energy. It is this line of energy that enables us to interact, communicate and guide you. It is the way we have always communicated with you. This link remains in place through the duration of your existence in the physical world. We have to tap into that link to make a connection. In fact, it is not only our abilities that enable us to communicate with you, but rather your strong connection to Dorna through your advancement and practice of meditation that enables you to have a strong connection, ultimately enhancing your ability to perceive us. The ability to feel our presence is not uniquely yours. It is an ability everyone can have. How often do you feel that you are being watched when no one is around? How often do you feel someone beyond your world is sending you a message? You all have this. You get those feelings when you are subconsciously in tune, not with us, but with your own line. And this feeling, this connection, can increase dramatically through practice of the mind.

Meditation?

Yes. And the power of imagination.

How exactly?

Meditation teaches you to quiet your mind. It teaches you to ignore the physical world and heighten the sensitivities of the brain that allow you to have a stronger, uninterrupted connection to your line. The power of imagination through the act of make-believe can generate powers and allow new thoughts that would otherwise remain restricted. If you approach any subject with a hard-nosed stubbornness, refusing to entertain a certain possibility, then that possibility will elude you. Like ghosts. If your approach to ghosts as if they do not exist, you will conclude as much no matter what evidence you find to the contrary. If you pretend, through the power of imagination however, that ghosts could exist, you act in a way that permits you to mentally accept such a conclusion.

You think it can be done?

Yes, we do. In fact, if you take it even further, and through practice act in accordance with our way of being – no emotions, no earthly senses – you will cause a great shift within your understanding there and your understanding here in Dorna.

Earth / Heaven Connection

Occasionally, I get a strong feeling that I need to do something, to go through an experience. Sometimes this experience is not exactly what I had in mind. Is it because of my connection to my spirit? An imprint of what I need to do?

It could be. It could also be an imprint of who you may have been.

Past lives?

Yes.

I don't really like the idea that spirits can tap into my line anytime they feel like it. I don't like the idea that spirits can manipulate me whenever they feel like it. I don't like it that I'm an open book for all of you to witness. Talk about invasion of privacy!

Privacy is a concept we have no use for here. We are not judgmental. We are not prone to the sensations of embarrassment. We have no need for secrecy. It is one of those things that can only be understood from here.

It seems we're a world away.

That is because you are. Furthermore, souls cannot be manipulated unless they allow themselves to be manipulated. An elevated soul's link to Dorna can only be accessed by elevated spirits. And elevated spirits have difficulties tapping into lower level spirits.

When you tap into my line and we converse, you're not here; you're there in Dorna. You're using my line like a fiber optic cable to transmit data between us, giving me the illusion that you are here. Is that right?

Well described. It is the only way for spirits like us to speak with you. We cannot directly exist in the physical dimension. It would destroy the spirit, the soul's only body. Or so we think.

I thought you said a spirit can't be destroyed.

We said that because there is no way for us to be present in the physical world without having a physical body. There has never been a case where a spirit crossed over. It is physically impossible; therefore, we can only assume that if it were possible, the consequences for the spirit body would be dire. However, what happens with the soul is a different matter altogether.

Why is that?

What happens to the soul should its only vessel in Dorna be destroyed we do not know.

Aren't ghosts basically souls without any body?

Yes, but a soul within the passage is still connected via its link to the spirit body in Dorna.

We've already discussed what happens to the soul once it decides to remain in the passage. Their connection is what scares me. The thought that a spirit can stay behind to avenge, for instance. Or perhaps I've just watched too many movies.

Any soul that has suffered or caused suffering and decides to remain in the passage because their connection to the physical world is strong will forget their reasons for staying behind within a matter of days due to their inability to receive energy. This delusional, energy-starved state combined with the trickery of the passage will negate any possibility of vengeance.

Who do the mediums actually speak to? They claim to see spirits. Are they ghosts? Are they souls that have been stuck in the passage or souls traversing the afterlife? Are they something else?

They speak to spirits in Dorna through their connections, and the images come into their minds via those links. But you are aware there are also many who *claim* to speak to the dead, but do not actually speak to any at all?

I would assume that to be true.

In ancient times, our communication stemmed from a need to improve humanity. Shamans, oracles and prophets would transmit the spirits' messages on deep philosophical matters to their followers. Modern times, on the other hand, have brought about a new breed of spiritualist – those who provide personalized messages from the spirit world to specific individuals that are fragmented and incoherent at best.

For as long as I could remember, way before I spoke to you, I didn't know what to make of the many mediums who claimed to speak to the spirit world. The spirits seemed to lack the ability to communicate properly or they had poor memories of the lives they once lived. For example, they could never get names right, picking only some of the proper letters from a first name or using a combination of names. I always thought, what happened to the spirits who once communicated with shamans and oracles in full, coherent sentences? Do we lose the ability to communicate when we die? Is the only way we communicate from the afterlife through pantomime? It certainly seems that way from the new age mediums who keep referring to the spirits' "gestures," such as pointing to the head or another body part in order to convey a message. Fortunately, the ability to fully communicate has not vanished, as you speak volumes, coherently and intelligibly, making it obvious to me that many mediums fake their communication through deceptive practices like "cold reading." By observing body language and other physical clues, the medium asks seemingly innocent but leading questions and provides vague statements that elicit a multitude of meanings. I wouldn't have problems with any of this if it were only for the sake of entertainment. However, these phony mediums are deceiving people for personal gain, toying with their emotions, adversely affecting predestined life experience, and giving the opposition legitimate grounds for attack.

We know this claim may sound a little hard to believe on its face, but you will not give a false sense of comfort by making others believe that a deceased loved one has contacted them in order to alleviate their grief, which is in fact a necessary part of their experience. Furthermore, it is not who we are (and we speak of all spirits at all levels), as we do not seek forgiveness or make things "right" with loved ones. It requires extreme amounts of energy to communicate with you, a skill not available to all spirits and definitely not readily available to the medium the moment he does his act.

Can ghosts communicate?

To some extent, yes. Earthbound spirits are at a stage in their existence that precludes them from actively participating in any medium's request let alone conveying messages that would provide closure for their human counterparts.

Are there real mediums today?

Yes, a few. However, their ability should not be treated as a conduit for sharing personal messages.

Any message for those who can communicate?

For fake mediums, our message is simple: do not lie and do not allow deception to become part of your path. Lies have an immensely negative effect on the spirit body in Dorna. If you are a true medium and the messages are not clear, then you are most likely speaking to Earthbound spirits, better known as ghosts. Although the messages may seem real, their lack of direction and clarity means it is better not to reveal them at all. However, if the messages are clear, rather than personal communication, join other mediums to deliver a universal message of spiritual renewal and prosperity.

It would be nice to make money from this connection.

We know you would not do that. But here is a message for you anyway. So long as it is within our ability, we will keep the messages flowing. Our messages will continue to be universal in nature and intended for the sole purpose of creating spiritual renewal and prosperity.

It is now the year 2017, five years after the promise of change and renewal that was supposed to come at the end of 2012. This alleged age of renewal was prophesized by the ancients and foretold by modern spiritualists. There are questions I keep hearing again and again. Like what happened to the change we were promised?

What if we told you it is already upon you? What if we told you there is no special alignment in the universe that allows for a new age?

There are so many people waiting for this new age of awakening. A period they call "Eden on Earth." Is it still coming? And if it's not coming, then what does await us?

Change is definitely upon us, but before we convey the message, dwell on this first: *no change shall come to you unless you become the change.* Allow this message to sink in for a moment. Many of you have been fooled into thinking that this change, this new age, would appear out of nowhere. Like magic. That it would just happen, assumedly during some special realignment of space and time. It is true that the universe rearranges itself on occasion and begins new periods, but in order to benefit from it, you are required to act.

I'm not sure I follow.

Take a community center dedicated to educating the children who enter its doors every day. A community center full of toys, games, art supplies, playground equipment and other educational tools. No matter how attractive that center is, the children must still make the choice to enter of their own free will. You see, even if the center is readily available as a tool of change, the children will never be able to take advantage of its many amazing features unless they walk through the door. It can be right near them, steps away, all the goodies there for the taking. But all those goodies will never step out of the center. They will never come to the children. The children must go to them. The universe is just the same. It has many community centers just like that dedicated to a variety of needs, and the good thing is that the doors never shut. They exist year-round. But just like a community center, you must go in. It will never come to you.

So, no matter how much we wait, spiritual growth will pass us by.

Do you really think that there is any process in the universe that simply comes to you? Even God's energy, which continually flows around you, requires great effort on your behalf to tap into it.

It's nice to think though that by doing nothing, the world somehow, at a predetermined calendar date, will automatically realign, and with it, realign who we are as well.

Like anything in the world, nothing will come to you. You must go to it. If you are unfit, you must exercise. And healthy food will not just appear at your front door; you must go get it. You will not suddenly find your brain chock full of information; you must educate yourself. Most importantly, you must build an apparatus to tap into all the energy around you.

So, 2012 wasn't anything special?

It was no different than any other year. A continuous period of spiritual growth is open year-round for everyone all over the world. All you have to do is enter the universal community center for spiritual growth, which will result in an ever-increasing strength in one's beliefs. Whichever path you take, whichever community center you enter, do it with all your might. The universe is neither prejudiced against nor partial toward any particular religion or spiritual movement. As a result, religious followers and spiritualists alike will gain an amazing comprehension of reality, especially when it comes to our purpose in this universe.

If I understand you clearly, you're saying that if those who partake in religious movements enter the universal community center, their understanding will be strong, which may open their eyes and their mind to new understanding.

It all depends on which part of the universe you embrace. It could very well open your eyes, or it could strengthen your already existing beliefs further. The universe is neither good nor evil. It has no say in the matter. The universe's energy can be a tool for development just as it can be a tool for destruction and stagnation. Unfortunately, the latter seems to come much easier.

How can the universe be good and bad at the same time?

Water can be both good and bad. It can be used to grow crops or create floods that destroy them. Water is necessary for a healthy physical body, but if you drink too much water, you can get water poisoning and die. There are many more things that fall into this category such as the sun or even human inventions.

I see.

The previous book, this one, and the next will all serve as a gateway for the community center the universe has to offer. It is for everyone. The future of our spiritual evolution depends on our actions, on us entering the many community centers the universe has to offer. It begins when you decide. It begins when you *wake up*! Educate yourself on the message we outline. You can become a leader in a revolutionary spiritual movement. An agent of change. A Pathian. Enlightened.

Mahatma Gandhi once said, "The future depends on what you do today." Sounds like pretty good advice.

The problem is that most of you will stay silent and do nothing. Most of you will remain in a dream-like state, placidly waiting for this magical new age to arrive. You will remain oblivious to the fact that this new age will never occur. Not that way anyway. We, on the other hand, cannot stand still. We will not wait for a magical period that never arrives. We will make the best of what the universe has already offered today.

I'm with you on this one. 2012 has come and gone, yet people are still sleeping. I'll do my best to wake them up.

You have our support and a message. There is no particular agent of change that will come to you unless you become that agent of change. If you want a spiritual transformation, then spiritually transform.

In the spirit of an Earth / Heaven connection, I was asked the following question: does candlelight have any relevance to our connection? For ages, many religions incorporated the tradition of lighting in some form – perhaps a fire through a sacrificial altar or through candles. I was asked this question by someone I know, and I sometimes try to answer questions based on the knowledge I already possess. Now, I know that the afterlife is flooded with light entering from other dimensions, and I might be wrong, but it seems to me that candlelight or any other light generated from a combustible product would be indistinguishable from the already wide variety of lights influencing your world. I can't imagine how you can distinguish the light of a candle from the light of the sun, for instance.

Not in human form you can't. All lights have a unique signature, making practically every form of light source visible to us. Lights are a very good method of reaching between our worlds, and candlelight – even as small as it may seem – becomes a beacon atop a lighthouse. It empowers your already established connection to the afterlife.

Interesting. So glad I mentioned to her that it was only my opinion, as I had yet to receive an answer from you on it. She will be happy to know that she was right in her thoughts, that there is a connection between the worlds and the use of candles. This brings me to a new question: if candles can serve as this beacon of empowering a connection between us, should we maintain even more elaborate methods of communicating with our spirit guides?

You are all communicating with us in one way or another.

I mean actual talking to you, like the way I do.

Not everyone will hear our replies.

Okay, then should we be talking to our spirit guides regardless of whether they speak back to us or not?

Not hearing us does not indicate that we do not speak back. In fact, we always speak back. You would be surprised at how easy it is to hear us. There is just one problem.

And that is?

Most of you do not ask us any questions. We hear people wishing for effects. We hear people asking for possessions. We hear people asking to get well. We hear people complain of their misfortune.

And the problem is?

We cannot give you any of this, nor will you receive it from God just because you ask for it. It does not work that way.

Then what are they supposed to do?

Ask us for the only thing we can truly give them. Answers. You have called us spirit *guides* for ages rather than spirit *givers* for the simple reason that we guide instead of give.

How will the answers arrive if they cannot hear you?

They will answer it for themselves through our guidance.

What you're saying is that they will answer their own questions, but in essence, how they come to those answers will be influenced and directed by you.

Yes.

I can see all the emails coming my way about how I'm in fact just answering my own questions.

Guided by our hands. What are you so afraid of?

That you're a figment of my imagination.

We drive and influence your imagination.

You have an answer to every question I ask.

We do not have an answer for every question (you know that very well), but for this one, we do: just let it be.

I'll have to. Otherwise, we'll go in circles about it.

We just want to be clear: do not expect your wishes to come true just because you ask. They will not. What we want to do is guide, and the only way we can do this is through your questions. That is it. We promise you will get your answers. Even if, in your mind, they feel like they are yours alone, they will be influenced and directed by us.

Do you want them to speak out loud, or can they talk to you in their minds?

Any way they feel comfortable. We do advise asking us questions under a meditated or relaxed state though, where the senses are not so overstimulated. It will enhance our ability to guide and their ability to perceive.

How can we trust our own answers, even under those conditions?

Because under these conditions, your answers will not only be guided by us, but also by your own body of knowledge contained within your spirit that is at all times accessible by you. In effect, you have to trust yourself more than you trust us. Subconsciously, you are always connected to the library of your life experiences saved within the spirit.

How will people know if they are truly guided?

They will simply know. A feeling. An intuition.

And I assume they can ask any question they wish?

Yes. You may ask any question you wish.

Any?

We realize where you are going with this, knowing you so well. But yes, we will answer any question. Allow us to elaborate. If you ask us what color shirt you should wear, you shall receive no guidance. However, if you truly want to speak to us, you shall receive a question that *you* have to answer, and in time, your answer to our question will eventually guide you toward the true question you were supposed to ask to begin with, to which you shall most definitely receive an answer.

How would you rephrase such seemingly trivial questions so as to align them with the requisites for your guidance?

Seeking advice on what shirt to wear derives from your sense of insecurity or fear of others' opinions or need for approval by others. There must be an inner reason for needing guidance on a level where guidance is actually not needed at all. You must search within through our guidance until you find the right question to ask.

I see. You must find the root cause behind your inability to make a simple decision.

If you wish to receive guidance from us, you must open your mind. You must allow the process of communication to happen. You must be honest with yourself because we will never be dishonest with you. Remind yourself that answers to all questions can be sought out with our guidance. Just never fall prey to the notion that there is an ultimate answer to a given question.

Why is there not an ultimate answer to a given question?

Because it depends on your point of view, and no matter how many points of view you may have, you will always miss many that are not within your grasp. For instance, take a building with four walls that are each painted a different color. When viewed from different sides or angles, you will get different answers to the question, "What color is the building?" Now, even if you have viewed all the sides of the building, you may have yet to view the building under different light or through the eyes of an animal or via other apparatuses that may skew the answer in other directions.

I'm pretty sure some questions have a definitive answer.

Like one plus one equals two.

Yes. That would be a perfect example.

Nature has been defining this question in many ways over time, proving that one plus one can yield different results. In fact, it remains an ever-evolving answer.

Do guiding spirits come from all planes?

Yes, they do.

So, the guidance will reflect the planes from which the spirit guides originated?

Indeed.

Then what's the point if they are just guided back to the same old, same old?

Your future does not lie in the hands of your spirit guides alone. It does not lie within the environment where you were brought up. It lies within your soul. Your soul is made up of Godly material and is able to observe or reject the energy around it. It is not limited by anything other than itself. Just like God's energy, which can traverse the universe regardless of its density, so can the soul. No environment and no spirit guides have absolute power over the development of the soul. You are the one that controls it. And your future.

Then why should we bother to talk to any spirit guides at all for that matter?

Because the act of speaking to your spirit guides helps you to evolve, regardless of what plane they occupy. It opens a line of communication to which you are privileged. It opens your sense of curiosity, which is the underlying essence of imagination, and subsequently the essence of your spiritual development.

How long have you been guiding us?

Since the time we realized we could progress faster through intervention, which was a very long time ago. You might say right from the beginning, or at least as far back as we can remember.

You realize, through your guidance and our interpretation of it, you've created many legends, myths and religions. And you still create more. Perhaps it's time for the Heaven / Earth connection to be severed so that things can stand as they are.

It is human nature along with the spirit nature, driven by the soul, that inherently remains the same in both locations. Yes, we all contributed to the ill fate of today's world, and it is through our evolution that we know we cannot stand still or sever the Heaven / Earth connection. In fact, we must strengthen it so we can undo all the damage that has been done. You must understand that every one of us here truly believes, regardless of the plane it exists on, that the message sent is the right message. But we sometimes forget one thing: the soul in human form behaves in completely different ways than its spirit body in Dorna. The soul in human form tends to make up a lot of stuff. The great sages once said, "What you don't see with your own eyes don't witness with your mouth." This is a kernel of wisdom we begrudgingly agree with, as it is the true source of many legends, myths and religions created on Earth.

How can we correct this?

By talking about it. By writing books and articles about it. By continuing what we are doing now.

I've received some answers through images while in my sleep. Am I one of a few, or is it something we all get?

Everyone receives guidance and answers to their questions in their sleep. It is during this time that the connection is the strongest, and if it was not for the fact that the mind is designed to forget when you awaken, you would remember more. This design is perhaps put in place to intentionally prevent the body from having full access to all its past lives and memories.

I find having a notepad next to my bed helps in documenting the images of a dream. Some mornings when I wake up, I find my writing is quite perplexing. On occasion, I can't even make sense of what I've written let alone make a connection to any tangible reality.

The moment you wake up, you lose memories. Even if you can recall some, the vast number of memories surrounding this memory vanishes. The reason we think this is by design and not a flaw is because other than subconscious guidance from us, whatever guidance you can consciously recall is always masked by the chaotic ways of the passage.

Speaking of messages received while in the passage, you said we all receive messages while we are asleep. What kind of messages are we getting?

Personal messages, universal messages, advice, warnings. Before you go to sleep and start documenting all the messages you are receiving, a word of warning: it is very important never to take the messages at face value. The passage is quite chaotic, and any message filtering down is broken into fragments rearranged in a manner that may seem confusing or even deceiving. It is important to make sense of the messages by putting the various puzzle pieces together in a way that aligns with the same understanding you already possess.

Why is it that way?

Messages that originated within Dorna nevertheless need to traverse the chaotic state of the passage in order to reach the soul. They pass through the vortices that dominate the passage, distorting and fragmenting them into pieces that are at times extremely hard to interpret by the confused soul. We have seen the consequences of such action. But understanding how the passage works allows you to understand the nature of the transmitter – that messages may not come through clearly or as intended. And though messages received through dreams need to be untangled, it still remains the easiest and best way to communicate between Dorna and the physical dimension.

You said that in order for me to piece together the message, I need to "align it with my understanding." What do you mean by that? What if the message is from a spirit who is not aligned with my understanding?

We are your guiding spirits, but under our shared obligation take the form of a single guardian spirit. Your soul (through the physical body) is guided by us, and your spirit body link to the soul is guarded by us.

I thought there was nothing to protect? That my spirit body is secure?

Your spirit body is very secure, but not the line to the soul. You are still prone to receive manipulative messages or nudges through the link. It is not to say that you can easily be manipulated by anyone else, however, as our combined efforts are meant to endure any deviation from our plans unless such an experience is in fact needed.

How about our connection?

Done in a different way, one that causes our communication to occur in short bursts.

I've noticed that. Why do we communicate over such short periods of time? Why not make it lengthier so we can complete more?

Because we must; otherwise, we will have a profound and adverse effect on you. A byproduct of being connected to Dorna's energy vibrations is that it brings a sense of calamity, which lies in contrast to what we are trying to achieve, what we want you to be.

Like being happy with what I have. Abandoning materialism. Not wanting to push myself further. Not wanting to advance.

Yes, that is what we are not trying to achieve. And that is not what you want to be.

I think I'm halfway there. I'm quite happy. If my life ended today, I don't think I'd have many regrets.

We know. That is why we must limit our sessions.

What do you want me to be?

We want you to be alive. To feel the need to explore, to challenge yourself, to be hungry for something, to create.

Perhaps you should stop talking to me.

This is your challenge, your correction. It is the correction of all those who are Pathians.

You explained in the first book that family like we have on Earth is not the same as in Dorna. That we have no gender and that there are no familial relations such as father, mother, son or daughter as there are here. Why is that? Why is it that we cannot continue over there the bonds that we have here?

Imagine if every family member that ever existed was united in Dorna – mother, son, grandson, great grandson, great great grandson, and so on and so forth. The amount of spirts united at the top would eventually be infinite. Do you see what we are getting at? Also, think about this. What if your father was your son and your son was your father? How would you establish the connection here? Who is the son? Who is the father? What if your father or your son and daughter are not aligned with your plane? What then? We understand emotional ties with your earthly family hamper you from even conceiving of the notion that you could live without them, but trust us when we say your point of view changes in an instant the minute you arrive here. We are not trying to be harsh. We are, after all, your family. And since we have been in your place before, we wholeheartedly understand you. Having a family and making memories with them will always be a part of you; however, in the grand scheme of it all, it is the opposite manner in which God exists.

In my effort to align myself with God, am I going to end up alone like Him?

Who said God is alone?

You just said having a family is opposite to how God exists.

God is alone, yet He is not. Confusing, we know. We have been there ourselves – in that elusive place trying to understand certain aspects of the universe that appear to contradict themselves. Here, in the spirit body on the seventh plane, we have come to the realization that one day we will likely find ourselves in the same contradictory situation as God: alone, but not alone. Yet we do not dread it. Rather we anticipate it with respect. We trust in the nature of our creation, made by a very meticulous and thoughtful Creator.

Chapter **9**

God and the Afterlife

Every person, in particular those who have faith, believe that one day they will be in Heaven, which is code for "the good afterlife." They will be in the presence of God and other religious figures who have played a significant role in the past. Most people imagine God as an old, white, bearded man walking amongst the clouds. I find it rather cliché that we use a human figure to explain what God is and don't have the power to imagine something beyond such a limited vision. How would you describe God? If not as described above, what is your understanding of what God is?

Though we know a lot about Him, on a larger scale, we know so little of Him. God cannot be defined, although if we had to, we would describe Him as a plurality and not a single entity. He can control matter and non-matter in and through observable and non-observable space and, of course, through time. God is both good and evil, darkness and light.

There are several arguments about God – in particular His abilities. One is that He's omnipotent; but if He is, then why allow evil to exist at all? If He can't stop evil, then He's not omnipotent. And if He can eradicate evil completely but won't, then what?

There was a time when we did not understand God's ways, so we intervened in every way possible so as to affect everyone's evolution. Now we know better. Only through guidance and free will can and will a spirit develop, and God in His own way is doing just that. This led us to the very basic conclusion that

God is both good *and* bad, yet He is simultaneously neither good *nor* bad. Bear with us. God is a seed planter. He allows things to grow and evolve through His predefined influence, but also by their own free will. He does not intervene in our affairs. Good and evil in the world are a product of that free will. Both can advance the soul, but only evil will advance you down a path that is harmful and isolated from God.

How can you advance through evilness and how does it isolate you from God?

Whether we like it or not, you can advance yourself in any direction you so choose.

But if God is both good and bad, how does being bad take you further away from Him?

Though God contains both qualities, His nature as a seed planter allows the very thing that those who choose evilness as their path do not exercise.

Free will, right? Evilness can't survive if free will flourishes among those it wishes to harm or control.

Exactly.

It's sad that we have free will, even in the presence of goodness, yet only a few choose to exercise it properly. Even though most people don't like being told what to do, when it comes to religion, they can't help but suppress the natural gift they've been given. It's time we stop attributing all the evil in the world to unseen powers and instead accept it as our own doing.

It is so hard for many of you to attribute evilness to human behavior that you have invented a scapegoat in the guise of Satan, blaming all bad things that ever happen on him. Many of you ascribed Hitler with evil qualities akin to the supernatural, even going so far as to call him the devil incarnate, but the fact of the matter is that Hitler was just a man. That should be scarier to you than any monster because it is easy to identify a monster; but a man capable of evils like this can look like any one of you.

He ate, drank, socialized with family and friends, and loved his pet dog. The horrendous capacity for evil that Hitler embodied is lurking within countless human beings today. We fear that.

I fear that, too. Now you've mentioned that God is both light and darkness. We've associated darkness with evil while speaking about the light as our salvation.

A wrongheaded notion stemming from your inability to comprehend that God can be both opposites at different times and at the same time. The argument must be laid to rest that if God is omnipotent and allows evil to exist, He is evil himself, but if God cannot eradicate evil, He is not omnipotent. New facts about God should be introduced. God *is* omnipotent, He's both good and evil, and He does not interfere in our journey other than the seed He has laid for us.

Some who have read my articles but not the first book have concluded that I don't believe in God. Yet throughout my life, I've never once doubted His existence. Though I rejected the description provided by the holy books, and couldn't come up with a description for Him myself, I've always believed in Him as an entity who creates. Just unlike any religious book has ever described His creations before.

And you believe He is a creator because…?

Because I can create.

Because you can create *and* because you must let go of your creation at one point, just as God does with us. Such reasoning brought us to believe that once our children have matured, they should be left to their own devices without interference from us.

You are intervening with us right now.

We do not intervene in your affairs; we guide. We simply set you on the right path, the one you have chosen. God does not intervene in our affairs, but He still sets us on the right path by way of his natural and absolute laws.

Do you think God will ever talk to us?

God is talking to us.

I meant like it's portrayed in the Bible.

No. It is hard to explain why not, as you must take the form of a spirit to understand. We communicate with Him through the strong connection we have with His particles. Basically, we cannot have a one-on-one conversation with Him, but we can say that He is talking to us through means other than His universal laws. Unfortunately, we have yet to advance sufficiently so as to interact with Him on a personal level. We all have this deep need to be able to speak to God in this way, but always remind yourself that we are speaking to an entity whose reach, understanding and abilities go far beyond anything imaginable. We are at the infancy of our development. We are to God as ants are to us.

You keep referring to God as a male. Is He?

We do not know. We believe He is genderless like us. All hypotheses lead to that conclusion. We refer to Him in the masculine as a matter of pure convenience and no other reason whatsoever, the same way you refer to us, though we are genderless, too. Within the body of the spirit, there is no limitation of language, and therefore we do not refer to Him as God either. He does not fall under any known description you have ever given Him throughout time.

I'll never forget the first time I dared to question my faith in my religion. I was unable to shake this confusion as to why God gave us the ability to think independently, yet according to the scriptures, demand we not use it. It was obvious to me from an early age that such a gift must *have a purpose, which brought me to the later realization that organized religions have simply shut the door on innovation. I think this is going to be another interlude where I start venting my frustration about religions. My religion of birth is Judaism, which contains 13 principles of faith. One of those principles is that there shall be no other Torah (the first five books of the Bible), which is the foundation of Judaism. This one simple principle creates an environment that impedes the evolution of the other principles of Judaism and ensures the religion can never be changed as long as that principle is upheld. It was told by Moses Maimonides (an influential rabbi and Torah scholar in the Middle Ages) that the Torah is unchangeable and will never be replaced by another. He claims this based on his own interpretation and not the actual words of God. The claim that the Torah is eternal, absolute and imperishable, even by an omnipotent God, contains many holes. The need that religions have to maintain the status quo stems from the idea that a change in religious doctrine will invite suspicion in the mind of its followers. By preventing new revelations, ideas and truths, they've protected themselves from the eventual embarrassment of having to explain why the God of the Bible will not make any new appearances. Restricting revelations to a preapproved canon also helps avoid the need for creating modern, innovative ways to interact with God on a personal level.*

They have also complicated the role of salvation by connecting it to the return of a Messiah who never existed to begin with.

Ohhhh, don't get me started on that! The return of the Messiah who's supposed to lead us into the afterlife? I wonder where they came up with such an idea! Moreover, the stipulations for his return have been complicated over time, further diminishing the likelihood that this event will ever happen. For the sake of argument though, let's assume the Messiah is real and in a hidden location waiting for all the conditions to be just right before he actually makes his appearance. What would it take for him to come? According to Jewish tradition, the Messiah will return when he's needed most (a statement widely open for interpretation), but the following conditions have also been suggested over time: if Israel repented a single day; if Israel observed a single Shabbat properly; in a generation that is completely guilty or completely innocent; or in a generation that loses hope. These conditions have evolved, not by what the Bible states, but by religious leaders' interpretations. According to Christianity, only when all conditions are met will Jesus return. The date for these conditions is not mentioned in the Bible and has been open to radically different interpretations itself. Necessary conditions include wars and rumors of wars, famine, pestilence, earthquakes and floods, one world government, the people of Israel returning to their land, and an overall increase in wickedness among mankind. I would argue that the conditions for the Messiah's return in accordance with Jewish and Christian teachings have been met time and time again, yet the Messiah is still not here. If our purpose is the afterlife and there is a way for the Messiah to help, why wait until the levels of wickedness have reached such an uncontrollable state? Why not just do it? Why not just arrive and show us the way?

If you never really believed in the return of the Messiah, why ponder so much on it?

I never believed for a second that it was God who set the conditions for the return of the Messiah. I never even believed the Messiah was real. I've always suspected it was religious leaders who came up with these impossible conditions to ensure they would never have to reveal to their followers their erroneous conclusions about his arrival. The magnitude of such events would be irreparable, of course. If all the conditions above were met and the Messiah still didn't make an appearance, rather than except the truth for what it is, I guarantee religious leaders and their followers would search their holy writings for passages that could explain away what happened while simultaneously extending the timing and further complicating the conditions for his return. I ponder all this because I want to understand why people think this way. Why can't they ask questions the way I and many others do?

This is not news. Complicating belief systems are not the only way religions have taken steps to ensure they shut the doors on innovation.

How else?

By repudiating the validity of mediums and psychics, which hinders you from receiving communication from the great beyond. They argue that the days of prophets and seers have long since passed; therefore, anyone who speaks with spirits today is deceiving or being deceived. Now that their religion is an established and bona fide powerhouse, they need no additional words from God or the spirits, particularly if the message serves to challenge the status quo. Rather than embracing knowledge from beyond this world, they choose to accept as truth the ancient stories that defy rationality while banning any further revelations, all the while concluding God does not want us in touch with spiritual beings.

Does God want us to communicate with the afterlife? Do you think our communications will have His blessing? Before you arrived, my inquisitive mind used to come up with so many questions. One persistent question was, why is the God of the Bible so afraid of giving up His grip on knowledge? Per Adam and Eve, why is He so apprehensive about our acquisition of knowledge? If that was the case, an omnipotent God could simply make it so that inter-dimensional communications were impossible. He could guarantee that no prophets, mediums or psychics would ever have a way of making that connection. We would simply not be able to communicate with the afterlife. But my gut is that the true God is not worrying about this at all.

His creation has a purpose. He does not make mistakes. It is not God who is worried that the conversations are taking place, but rather religious leaders who wish to prevent their followers from ever obtaining new knowledge in order to maintain them as a source of wealth.

Why don't they question instead of submitting? Why don't they lead instead of follow? Why don't they want to advance?

Furthermore, let's assume for a moment that the Messiah (or Jesus for that matter) will return. If that did happen under today's conditions, he would definitely be crucified. Not literally, but by the people and, more specifically, through the media. This blockade of new ideas has inevitably shut the door on the possibility of such a return.

I understand all you have ever told me about God is based on your connection to Him and, in particular, your intuition on the matter. I trust your opinion more deeply than I would trust any holy book, so on this same subject, I would like to ask you what God says about communicating with the afterlife through channeling or mediums? Now, it would be wise to differentiate between the real God's answer and what the God of the Bible says. I know the God of the Bible is very much against it, which is in total contradiction to all that I've already learned from you. Leviticus 19:31 (NIV) says, "Do not turn to mediums or seek out spiritists, for you will be defiled by them." This doesn't take a genius to understand it, but when it comes to any writing, you must always read it in its original language. Not that it lends more validity to the argument, but it will show the mindset of the person writing it, as it's the tendency of human nature to exaggerate, extrapolate or interpret in ways that coincide with their agenda. And so, I did read the original. To my surprise, I found that in accordance with Hebrew, Leviticus 19:31 should be read as follows: "Do not turn to the fathers and unto those who are knowledgeable, do not ask to be defiled by them." This is not my interpretation, but rather my reading straight from the Hebrew Bible as it was meant to be read. After all, the Bible was originally written without the misinterpretations that were later made up to serve a certain agenda. The translated word "mediums" is a word that repeats many times in the Bible, only it describes "fathers." The translated word "spiritists" is also a word that repeats many times in the Bible, only it describes different forms of "knowledge." Regardless of whether you interpret it as you want or read it as it's supposed to be read, the agenda of religious leaders is to ensure that you shouldn't put your trust and reliance in fathers (which at the time had more influence), mediums, spiritists, or those who are considered "knowledgeable." The need to abstain from all other sources of knowledge is further emphasized in Deuteronomy 18:9-12 (NIV), which says, "When you enter the land the Lord your God is giving you, do not learn to imitate the detestable ways of the nations there. Let no one be found among you who sacrifices their son or daughter in the fire, who practices divination or sorcery, interprets omens, engages in witchcraft, or cast spells, or who is a medium or spiritist or who consults the dead. Anyone who does these things is detestable to the Lord." Agreeing wholeheartedly with the sacrifice part, the rest sounds like a conspiracy to prevent messages from above. Now, one might ask, if the Biblical God is true, why is He so afraid of these types of communications? And if He fears it so much, why can't he put a lid on it? Okay, now that I've ranted and sidetracked, I'll go back to my original question. What does the true God say about communication with the afterlife through channeling or mediums?

In contradiction to what we have established between us through this communication, and in contradiction with spirits from the lower planes who do not share the same opinion, we strongly believe that God's intent was that there be no communications between Dorna and the physical dimension.

How did you arrive at that conclusion?

In the way we are precluded from remembering our past lives. There is a reason we do not remember. The same reason you struggle to align with your spirit's energy, which stores all your memories. For the reason it is hard. For the reason most of you fail to comprehend us.

So why are we communicating?

Because of the actions of all those who do not abide by this universal law. You see, the warning by the Bible, though given to serve an agenda, is in fact justifiable to some extent. Let's exclude for a moment the risk associated with fake messages given by fake channelers and mediums. Even true channelers and mediums are deceived into thinking they are communicating with spirits residing in Dorna while in fact they are speaking to Earthbound spirits whose message is disoriented and deceitful due to the chaotic nature of the very medium they travel upon: the passage. It is messages received within the confines of the passage that wreak havoc on the development of the soul. Messages that are not questioned for their truthfulness are dangerous messages for the taking. These are messages that only few dare to question.

Why does it have to be deceitful?

Earthbound souls trapped within the passage are not purposely deceitful. They are disconnected from their spirit bodies, influenced immensely by the last lives they lived where their fears become reality, and furthermore deprived of their energy, making them unable to see their new reality for what it truly is. Every piece of knowledge they provide is an unintentionally distorted message of what Dorna is.

Then the Bible is right in regard to communication?

The Bible is right, but it does not condemn or question the revelations' origins by the prophets that are the basis for Biblical beliefs. People who claim to communicate with dead relatives in Dorna are receiving deceitful messages that can serve to harm spiritualism. You should always question communication with Dorna. It is, we admit, a bit unfair and hypocritical to ask others to reject information from above while an old way is accepted without question.

Is that why you ask no one to automatically believe in your message?

It is the only logical thing to ask. Always question the truth. Always question the messages you receive. Both the old and the new.

Then back to my earlier question. Why are we communicating? Why not adhere to this universal law and remain silent?

Those who have unintentionally broken this rule caused us to shift our intended purpose in the wrong direction. If people, based on old communications, once ventured into valleys, and based on new communications seek to venture there no more, then it is exactly to the valleys we must go.

The Bible says of the dead, "For the memory of them is forgotten. Also, their love, their hatred, and their envy have now perished." It's saying that we should not seek to communicate because the dead know nothing nor feel anything. The part about losing your memory does not describe you at all, as you remember plenty; but the second half describes you more or less, as you do not love, hate or envy. The claim seems to be that the essence of what once made you human is held against you when the living seek you out for guidance.

We hold so many memories of so many lives, and it is through this fact alone that we can guide you in the right direction. Losing our humanity when we become spirits residing within Dorna should not be confused with a lost soul in the passage, nor should it constitute a weakness in our judgment.

By the sheer fact that you freed my mind, made me question, asked me to doubt all and trust in myself is enough for me to know that your message is the one I've always longed for. I always felt I should be the judge of what to believe and what not to believe, and that I shouldn't allow anyone to dictate it to me. In my opinion, the Biblical God shouldn't be threatened by channelers. Furthermore, an omnipotent God shouldn't have left a back door of communication open if He didn't wish for this alleged blasphemy. I think, as I always did, that this is all a man-made creation to restrain followers from finding truth and independence. The only way to restrain followers as Leviticus 20:27 (NIV) says is through threats to a person's life: "A man or woman who is a medium or spiritist among you must be put to death."

To constrain a soul, you make it afraid. And although we believe that communications should not be made, we do not want you to think that communicating between Heaven and Earth should be construed as a bad or good thing. We live in God's creation, and we do not think we have the right to judge whether communications on all levels from all planes of Dorna, including the passage, are good or bad.

See, this is where you lose me. You conflict yourself.

Nothing ever goes in a straight line. Confliction is part of the Pathian way. Look at God's creations on Earth. He has given you a land flowing with milk and honey, yet He also created the simple and undesirable weed, "a plant in the wrong place" with no botanical significance at first glance. These weeds grow and reproduce aggressively and can survive in harsh and diverse environments. Weeds may seem bad from your initial perspective, but they can enhance soil fertility, making them good as well. So, if something such as a weed can be both good and bad at the same time, communications between Heaven and Earth can be as well.

I'm on the side of good when it comes to our communications and your messages. However, others would disagree because it is not aligned with the communications and messages from the God that is portrayed by the holy books.

It is hard to believe in a transcendental being when it is not aligned with human experience. Holy books are filled with descriptions of God as if He is somewhat of a human being, but He is not. When you realize the shortcomings of religions and how their inhibiting beliefs cripple you, how they compromise your existential connection and understanding of God, Dorna, and the universe in general, you will realize the real reason why you are here in this life. And when that happens, your mind will be unshackled from its constraints, setting free the very thing that will enable you to believe in a transcendental being and His message.

Chapter 10

The Voices

Did you ever try speaking to me before? I swear I'd heard voices calling my name when I was young. I'd be alone in a room and hear a whisper in my ear.

In your mind.

Was it you?

It was.

This is weird.

What is?

I've heard my name whispered in my ears for a long time, and—

You have heard your name whispered in your mind.

It feels the same. I've heard my name whispered in my mind for a long time, and it's as clear in my memory as a sunny day. Whether I was in a room or outside in public, I'd be looking in the direction of the sound only to see no one. What's weird is that back then, I assumed it was my imagination, but I always had a feeling someone or something was around me. Still, why did I not once answer back? I had nothing to lose by answering the call. I'm trying to put a finger on it. I'm just not sure why I held back. Now that you speak to me in full sentences, I'd like to know what I am. Am I a medium? A prophet? A messenger? A writer?

You are not a medium. *We* are the ones who established the connection with *you*. You are not a prophet either. What are prophesies anyway? There is no God-ordained destruction looming over you other than the natural events you are already aware of.

Then what am I?

You are a messenger.

I don't feel like a messenger. I'm nothing but a writer. A writer whose words direct, liberate and advance the soul. I'd rather have this label than "messenger." This is my mission. I've become a writer of your words.

You keep fighting the idea that those words are something other than your own. Why?

I think words coming from you will have more weight to them.

This message was always yours. We are just here to remind you of it. You remain both the messenger and the originator of the message. You question your role a lot, but question why this message resonates so loudly within you. Because it is *yours*.

It's just really hard for me to see myself as a messenger, but I'll go along with what you say. Now that I know who and what I am, I've realized I still don't know who you are.

As we told you before, we are who we are.

But who are you really*?*

We are Pathians just like yourself. Spirits who have no names. If you mean who we were in the physical world, we believe that has no importance to who we are now. Who we once were is just an experience that will forever remain with us.

I understand your stance on the matter, I truly do, but it's just that I, like the readers, would like to associate great figures from our distant past with the messages they convey.

We understand. So then, would you be disappointed if we were not important figures from the past?

Honestly, I'm not sure if I would be or not. Your message has been great regardless. But I assume that if you were someone special from the past — someone on the magnitude of a king, queen or prophet — it would mean something, though I can't put my finger on exactly what that would be.

You give so much importance to characters from the past that you forget the present.

Many of us embrace the ideas behind those people of the past.

Yet many of you willingly delve right back into the chaos created by ancient ideologies of the past as well. No person in history has the power to change the world if the world will not change. Answer us this. Who are you really?

I'm a messenger.

You are, but who are you?

Guy?

Yes, but *who* are you?

I'm starting to get confused here. What are you getting at?

Your identity, what you call "you," is just an idea of who you think you are. However, at any given moment, if you chose to, you could shed your identity, throw it away and get a new one. If you just see yourself differently without ever thinking of how others see you, you can do wonders for yourself. Furthermore, you remove the need to ask, "Who am I?" "Who are we?"

So, you're an idea.

For now, this is who we are. This is the idea we are embracing. It is not a name that defines us, but what and who we stand for.

Hillel the Elder said, "If I'm not for myself, who is for me? And being for my own self, what am I? And if not now, when?" It is amazing that this knowledge was understood and available to us a long time ago, yet we constantly choose to ignore it. It puzzles me.

It puzzles us, too.

So, I'm an idea. It's hard to accept.

Your body changes 100 percent of its atomic particles every year. So, you can say for certain that whoever you are, it is not who you were a year ago. In addition, your body is approximately 72 percent water combined with heavy elements like carbon, sodium and potassium. Is that what defines who you are? You are an idea, a concept embedded within the soul, able to advance and evolve as you choose. Do you understand who you are now?

An idea. I am what I am. But I've seen your images, your faces.

This is not who we are. It is simply how we want you to see us.

I've seen you and I'm perplexed as to why you chose faces that aren't perfect. Not to say I didn't like the way you look. As a matter of fact, I like it more than a perfect face. But you all could have chosen any faces you wanted to, and yet you chose those.

What is perfection?

Well, for one, humans are by nature prone to be attracted to anyone's face that follows the golden ratio, which is the ideal result. According to this measure, a beautiful person's face is about 1.6 times longer than it is wide. Of course, there other details as well, but this is the general standard of facial perfection as we consider it.

And who decides what human behavior is naturally prone to?

Evolution?

You liked our faces even though they do not fall into the criteria of what you are led to believe is beautiful because you evolved beyond the restrictions of what others abide by. The natural and absolute laws of God do not apply to human behavior, and so we can break away from behaviors that are programmed into the biological brain.

Which brings us back then to that same idea of identity. That regardless of what face I have or what voice I have, I am what I decide I am.

Well said.

I know I've inquired about your past life identities many times, but curiosity gets the better of me, and so I must ask, once I pass, will I recognize you? Will I know who you are and who you were?

You will know it all. Us, you and much more.

I still sometimes think you are nothing but a lucid dream.

We thought we settled this a long time ago.

I guess it's the fear that lies deep inside of me, wanting to make sure that I'm on the right path. I can't explain it, but when I'm in your presence, I know for certain this is right. However, the minute I'm alone, questions and uncertainties arise.

Which is perfectly fine. Do not forget that we encourage you to ask, and we encourage skepticism, even if it is directed toward us. These are attributes that prevent you from stagnating and drive you to higher ground.

Are you Arcturians?

Where did that question come from?

Were you expecting it?

We came to realize at one point, either by your digging or by questions sent to you, that this question would become inevitable.

I've received a few questions from readers that centered around this theme – one in particular that grabbed my attention. I must say although I like to read a lot, I don't recall ever running into the subject of Arcturians. Now, being the Pathian that I am, I was obliged to do some research, and I must say I was amazed at the similarities between you and the Arcturians; so much so, that I don't feel it's a stretch to logically conclude that you are one and the same. Got to love those questions! People are so curious and knowledgeable, and the questions they ask teach me a great deal. They force me to look things up, which I did in regard to this matter, of course. Before I tell you what I found, just a little fact about my search. I couldn't find the origins for the knowledge behind the Arcturians, but the internet seems to be teeming with information about them. Arcturians are supposed to be higher beings who exist mostly on a spiritual plane settled by pure thought and consciousness. Their central belief system is a philosophy of healing and compassion. They are described as three to four feet in height with greenish-blue skin and unmistakably large, oval eyes. They have an average life span of 350 to 400 years, and their entire life's purpose is spiritual development. They are known to be the most intellectually acute and caring species in existence. They remain hidden, serving as the guardians of Earth, transcending between the fourth and fifth dimensions. The Arcturians do not eat like we do; rather they consume positive forms of energy. I've found many things about them, but the one thing that caught my attention was their telepathic abilities, enabling them to instantly communicate with humans across the galaxy. Sounds like you. So, are you Arcturians?

If we were Arcturians with telepathic abilities, don't you think it would benefit us to send a telepathic signal that encompassed the entire Earth, reaching billions of people all at once? Can you imagine the effect it would have?

You still didn't answer my question.

We do not live on a spiritual plane. We live in a dimension with a multitude of planes. We do not exist as "pure consciousness," whatever that means. Our central belief system is not a philosophy of healing and compassion, but rather one of freeing your mind so you can heal yourself and, therefore, will never need compassion. We do not have physical bodies and our life span is eternal (at least for now). Our entire life is not spent on spiritual development, but rather the evolution of our entirety, including spiritual development. We are not hidden; you are simply unable to see us. And we are not guardians of the Earth. We are who we are. We feed off energy, but it is not distinguished by positive and negative. Most importantly, we do not communicate across the galaxy, but rather across dimensions. In short, we are not Arcturians.

Are Arcturians real?

Arcturians are not real.

Sometimes I think the questions I ask sound silly or even dumb. I ask questions that I don't even believe can be true—

But you ask nevertheless. The truth is that there are no silly questions and there are no dumb questions when you seek knowledge. Our notion of what is silly or dumb or ridiculous has been influenced for too long by the status quo. So, in the end, as a Pathian, as a seeker of knowledge, it is better to ask the question, regardless of its attributes, than to sit quietly and ponder what answer may lie beyond your muteness.

Okay, so I have to ask the following question as well because I can see the emails coming my way. I asked if you're Arcturians, which is more of a specific alien race, but doesn't include the rest of the alien races. So, just to be safe, are you aliens of any sort? Pretty much any aliens who might have the technology to manipulate me into thinking you're spirits?

What if we were? Would your willingness to accept the message be any different if it came from aliens instead of spirits? What else would our agenda be if not freeing you from the chains of ancient beliefs? Have we ever asked you to do anything out of the ordinary, anything that would violate even one of the Ten Commandments as we discussed in the previous book? All that we ever asked – never demanded or insisted, just asked – was that you open and free your mind. We understand that some may see this as a dangerous thing, especially when it comes to defying established ideas. But to answer your question, the same one we have answered many times, we are you. We are spirits. We are a continuation of you. We have no reason to make up stories or lie to you when we never asked you to believe us in the first place. This explanation will perhaps confuse your understanding even further, but as stated before, not only are you

God, at least a part of Him, but you are also the alien you keep referring to.

You're right. You've confused me even further.

We will explain. You are accustomed to recognizing certain lifeforms that you are unable to see along with the intelligence in those lifeforms that you have no understanding of nor ability to recognize. We are talking about the phenomena that happen in the universe, from subatomic particles to dark matter to the driving forces behind quantum physics. If you were able to see us as we truly are, you would see we are nothing but a spec of energy engulfed by a driving force of external energy to which we and you call God.

So, you're saying that there could be aliens around us, only we're unable to decipher them, and they're literally us.

Yes.

Will we ever be able to see you directly, to decipher you?

Some sights and energies flow in one direction only. We believe that in the limited human form, you will never gain that sight. It is only through the spirit that we can broaden our understanding and abilities. However, perhaps a new stage will one day shed light on the most important question of our lives.

Who is God?

Yes.

And you think the eighth plane will broaden that knowledge?

We are certain it will further our understanding.

You know, I'm elated to go through this experience with you, but at the same time, my intellectual side can't stop entertaining the idea that you're simply a figment of my imagination, the product of an overactive brain that I could very well be using to manipulate myself.

What if it is?

Well, if it is… then all I've ever written of ancient and modern beliefs are simply the result of an overactive imagination. Yet even before our conversations, I couldn't shake the feeling that there was more to life than what we actually see. That's why I agree with you when you say rather than concentrate on things that can't be proven, concentrate on the importance of this book's message instead.

Amen.

I repeatedly ask you the same doubting question with only slight variations, yet you never get upset with me. Not even once have you told me to stop asking you the question. Not once did I sense through your voice that you were getting frustrated.

We are Pathians – spiritually advanced beings – and in accordance with that advancement, we do not get mad or upset. We thrive on questions and answers; therefore, we understand that development and evolution of the spirit rely heavily on understanding and knowledge. We are obligated to answer and continuously seek understanding ourselves through questions. Sometimes you may ask the same question many times and not allow the answer to sink in, not until it is asked the final time, and then it does. It is through this understanding that we are able to be so tolerant.

I wish I could do that myself, answer the same question again and again without showing signs of frustration.

You are hindered by the limitations of your physical body.

Yes, I believe I am. Is that why you asked me to write the book in the form of questions and answers?

Questions and answers are the essence of who we are. Without them, we would revert back to who we were during ancient times, stagnating our advancement.

I ask a lot of questions.

Yes, you do. In fact, a bit more than we expected.

The day you told me that my project and business failed because of your intervention, I decided that, as a punishment, I would make you guys work hard. I decided that as long as you allowed it, I would bombard you with an infinite number of questions. Might as well take advantage of this situation you all have put me through.

It is no punishment at all.

Do you ever ask questions?

All the time.

Who answers your questions?

Our advancement. We are always in pursuit of answers. In fact, we have so many questions to date that have yet to be answered.

It's hard for me to think about how a movement such as ours can succeed should people not follow. After all, the principle basis for every movement that ever existed is followers. Moreover, how do you unite people who do not follow? I had sent "111 The Path" to many publishers and agents in an effort to gain their help in promoting our message, and to my amazement, I was contacted rather quickly by several top publishers. At first, I would receive a plethora of positive feedback. There seemed to be tremendous interest. However, after several days of consideration, it was always rejected. They would give no good reason other than a brief phone call telling me that, despite how wonderful this message is, they fear it would cause an uproar among their faithful readers whose beliefs lie in contrast to the book's message.

They are afraid.

Of what? Of another point of view on the universe? Another point of view on who we should be?

Of losing business. "111 The Path" and this book, both of which have the same message, are not what you would call regular books.

It is a spiritual book. Many spiritual books have been written.

All spiritual books, even those that channel information like yours, acknowledge at one point (almost without exception) a connection to a Biblical figure such as Jesus Christ or a connection to a Biblical God. Our message, on the other hand, tells the truth as observed by us. Even though our message is a liberation to many, it is nevertheless also a message of destruction to many others who want to hold on to their beliefs.

One of the publishers was willing to publish it at first, but ultimately rejected it because I don't have a platform of followers. How am I going to have a platform when the very idea of having followers is anathema to our message?

It will be a platform. But a platform of a different kind. It will be one that releases you from the grasp of an utterly limiting physical body. One that liberates you from the constraining influences of others.

Though Jesus's words are often misunderstood, his platform has gained much momentum since his death. I just hope you don't expect me to die for people in order to free their minds... You're silent. Anything you wish to tell me?

We do not expect anything from you other than for you to continue writing.

How many books am I supposed to write?

How many years are you planning on living?

I'm not sure. What was my plan for this life?

To write.

I guess I'm just frustrated that this message has not gained the momentum I expected.

It is catching on fast.

Really?

Do not forget that time moves faster for us. The results are acceptable.

It'd be nice if the message was being received just as fast in my time. You say that our message liberates the reader and frees their mind, yet you call the same message a destroyer of other beliefs. I agree, but in a good sense. How can this message be so good and yet so bad? How can they not see the benefits of the good?

Years of holding onto one point of view clouds their vision. This one reason is the root cause for their refusal to allow the mind the freedom it so needs. Many periods throughout our history have seen good intermingling of viewpoints that ignited the continuing evolution of the soul. One period in particular was between 1883 and 1925 in New York City, when a staggering number of immigrants from many different countries with many different points of view arrived and were forced to share the same limited area. These immigrants often tried to maintain their own cultures, but at the same time found themselves in the midst of a cross-cultural intersection like they had never experienced before. Unable to turn off their curiosity, they gave respect and consideration to other points of view just as they asked for it themselves. What made New York special was the mix of ideas and traditions that piqued curiosities and in return gave rise to freer minds. That was the moment when New York became the great place that it is today. There is a problem though, which is quite unique to those who follow.

Which is?

That at times, even when great ideas are shared, a common ground that encompasses those ideas becomes the motivational force that eventually reduces diversity and drive.

Let me see if I got this right. As long as ideas remain free to be explored and debated outside the constraints of a single ideology, it's good; but if those separated ideas become united under one ideology, it's not.

That is why we are never to become a movement of followers, but rather a movement of *leaders*. Followers just follow. They do not generate new ideas. Leaders create ideas and other leaders, who then create more leaders and newer ideas, and so forth. The leader will retain his singularity, his individuality, as opposed to the follower who simply becomes one of a plurality.

You spoke of me as a leader, yet I don't see myself as one.

You are leading with a great message.

Your message.

You keep trying us on this issue. The message is *yours*. Always was and always will be.

Okay, so if I'm a leader, and our followers are not followers, but rather leaders, can a leader lead leaders?

A leader leads with leaders and leaders lead with the leader.

Are you messing with me?

We told you before, and it still stands true – you are a leader in charge of our great family here, but you are not alone in this leadership role. Perhaps a little explanation would help. You are not in charge per se, such as telling us what to do, nor would you ever allow us to tell you what to do, but what makes you in charge is your actions. You are a pioneer in this adventure, setting the standards and establishing a pattern of continuity. We look up to you. We learn from you and others like you, as you have been at the forefront for a long time, never stopping, never ceasing in your progress.

This is not the kind of leader you had me believe myself to be, but then again, there are so many new meanings I have to get used to. I'm therefore not surprised that there's some struggle against the belief that for a great movement to exist, we must all unite behind a great figure, someone we follow.

Which lies in total contradiction to the Pathian way.

Can a leader lead leaders and leaders lead the leader?

Yes. It would be a great path, one we would like to see. A great leaderless movement, as it should be.

This family in the afterlife is obviously not bonded by blood or love, but rather by a mutual interest in progression. You've said that love is not important. You've said you will give me one piece of advice that will shake the very ground I walk on as it relates to love. Many speak of love as if it were the most effective propellant to the afterlife.

Here is our advice: love is a great mechanism regardless of who it is directed at, but it is not what we long for. Love is an enslavement to the physical body, forcing you to act in often uncontrollable ways. Love is an attraction, a feeling of constant affection for a person generated by an internal mechanism that is out of your control. This internal mechanism has yet to catch on with the evolution of the soul. With time, however, the feeling will subside as, once again, the internal mechanism will dictate the continuation of the soul. But there is one other quality that *is* within the total control of the developed soul, one that should be considered far more important than the grips of love.

And that is?

Respect.

Respect?

Respect is the driving force that bonds us and differentiates us from others. We very much value respect in Dorna.

Why respect?

Because respect is within the control of the mind. It is a deep admiration for someone prompted by their abilities and qualities and achievements. Respect for others is based on the guidelines of our universal commandments. That is why those whose opinions differ from ours have our unbridled respect so long as those opinions are not enforced upon us. That is also why anyone joining us has to do so of their own accord. Moving up the planes requires the qualities, abilities and achievements of a leader.

If we could only achieve it here. That would be extraordinary.

Respect is not an easy thing to act upon. It requires thought. It requires seeing the world through others' eyes. It is an ability only gained by being a leader and not by being a follower.

How can this respect be achieved here? I mean I understand that my beliefs or the way I act should not interfere with the lives of others, and it should be reciprocal, but there are those around me who certainly can't seem to understand this concept.

Do not worry about fostering universal respect all over the world. That would be nearly impossible. We are merely seeking an increase in our numbers so we can move beyond our plane. We are not here to awaken the whole world.

Why not?

Well first, because we cannot. That is just reality. Second, there are forces working against us all the time, forces greater in number than we are. You see, we are at a distinct disadvantage. We cannot force believers into our plane; they must wish for it themselves. On the flip side, there are a great many others who simply force people into their beliefs, if not by physical force, then by superstition and the promise of great results in the afterlife.

We have such a disadvantage. It's most definitely easier to be a follower and be told what to do than be a Pathian and a leader who contributes to our understanding. If only it was the other way around — that good things would be easy while bad things would be hard. But then again, you already explained that good things aren't necessarily hard, and I agree with you. I just have to keep reminding myself that nothing, and I truly mean nothing, *is hard.*

Nothing is hard.

If you are energy, can you explain how myself and others are able to see spirits as if they are in human form?

The ability to manipulate you into seeing whatever we want you to see is quite an easy thing for us to do. We can also influence devices and imprint an image as we wish.

Why not show your true form?

We have. You are just unable to recognize us. Using forms with which you are familiar is the only thing that makes sense to you while you are in the physical dimension.

You spoke of a side effect that occurs as we climb up the planes. How can we repair it?

Simple. We must continue asking questions. And if there is no one to answer our question, we still must never give up on the search for that answer. There was once a father who was looking to marry his daughter to a fine man. He went to a town known for its intellectuals and promised to give his daughter's hand in marriage to whoever could solve a certain riddle before he departed in two days. The young men of the town all tried, but could not find the answer. Most simply gave up. After two days, when no one answered the riddle, the father got on his carriage and left for home. Just as he was about to exit the town, a young man, exhausted and breathless, managed to catch him and stop the carriage. "I did not sleep for the last two days," said the young man, "trying relentlessly to solve the riddle. I know I have failed and do not deserve to wed your daughter, but I must… I must know the answer to the riddle." The father looked at the young man with a smile and replied, "I don't know the answer to the riddle. I don't even know if there is one. But you are the only one who was curious to know the answer and therefore deserve to wed my daughter." Pathians should never be comfortable, but rather always driven to greater heights. Pathians should be persistent in their efforts to garner new knowledge. Just to be clear, we are not requiring Pathians to be researchers or scientists or discoverers of new knowledge. We only ask that they discover and familiarize themselves with the vast reservoir of knowledge that is already at our disposal.

We sometimes don't seek any new knowledge because we are limited by the belief that we are incapable of doing it or understanding it. In short, our beliefs are what limit us.

That is true. What you consider to be true, regardless of whether it actually is, is the cause of your limitations.

We can't help it, as it operates at a deep subconscious level.

Without addressing the causes for such behavior in this book, we will remind you that you are a Pathian, and are therefore capable of living your life in ways other than how you were told you should. And you are most definitely able to shift your mind or even empty it. Perhaps a fable by Anthony de Mello can explain it better. One day, a man found an eagle's egg and put it in the nest of a barnyard hen. The eaglet hatched with the brood of chicks and subsequently grew up with them. All his life, the eagle did what the barnyard chicks did, thinking he was a chicken. He scratched the earth for worms and insects. He clucked and cackled. He would thrash his wings, but fly just a few feet into the air. Years passed, and the eagle grew very old. One day, he saw a magnificent bird soaring above him through the cloudless sky. It glided in graceful majesty among the powerful wind currents, with scarcely a beat on its strong golden wings. The old eagle looked up in awe. "Who's that?", he asked. "That's the eagle, king of the birds," said his neighbor. "He belongs to the sky. We are chickens. We belong to the Earth." And so, the eagle lived and died a chicken, for that is what he thought he was. Just like the eagle, if you do not shed your limiting beliefs, you will never figure out what great things you are capable of. The reason you have not shed any beliefs is because you have become roundly accustomed to them, with little to no tangible interest in acquiring new knowledge. Your family and friends share your beliefs, and they would most likely turn their backs on you if you ventured outside that belief system. If you want life to be easy and approved by many, then you are not curious by nature and do not wish to evolve.

What must we do?

You must accept that all aspects of your life, including the religious parts, are at best a product of others. That you are currently eagles living the lives of chickens. To be an eagle, you must believe you are one. It is not going to be easy, but if you do, you will soar through the sky just like an eagle.

It's not as easy as you say it is. I know it firsthand. Knowledge caused me to abandon the pursuit of greatness in business, although it didn't stop me from being great with my family. The competition of daily life isn't a necessity for me anymore. It's for that reason that I can't promote the advancement of the Pathian movement fervently. I'm already beyond the need to argue with people about religious matters let alone share my knowledge (or you for that matter) with them. In a way, I may look selfish, but nevertheless, my understanding of who I am and what I am comforts me greatly.

You still have a lot to work on. And we are here to help you overcome those hurdles. The limitations of our success become the limitations of our continuation. We must always stay in touch with our purpose and overcome the physical body's hold on our behavior.

Can we speak about Edgar Cayce?

There will be a time for that. Not in this book though.

Why not?

Just trust us.

I will. In the meantime, let me ask you about some of the cults and weird, eccentric people who claim to speak to spirits or aliens. They're preaching ideologies that can be construed as evil. Do you have any knowledge about this?

Trickster spirits, or those you might call "evil spirits," communicate just as well as we do. Their ideology about existence lies in total contradiction to ours.

Is there such a thing as an evil spirit?

We are created in the image of God, and therefore both qualities, good and evil, are embedded within our souls. Evilness is a choice. Yet with good tools, we can overpower and suppress the evil side in us. The sad part is that it can happen the other way as well.

So, when did you decide that good was better than evil?

The day we started going that route was the same day the soul's abilities started rising greatly, while those who chose the evil route stagnated in place. We are all granted the ability to choose, and choose wisely we do, but in order to confront and handle evil, we must acknowledge that the source of this evil lies within each and every one of us. Understanding this concept means the act of excusing evilness with a cause other than ourselves is rather silly. Accept it, and you have in your hands the tools to deal with it properly.

How about demons?

No demons. Trickster spirits can be sufficiently evil so that you confuse them with demons. This, too, we shall speak of at another time. But for now, know this: no spirits can harm you in a direct, physical way.

I used to have this belief that I'm pretty sure at one point was shared by others. (Some may still.) It was a belief of our own creation. That if you kept your feet and hands within the boundaries of the bed, covered by blankets, you'd be safe from malicious spirits. It's as though we believe our blankets are the ultimate defense from evil – a magical shield preventing anyone or anything from crossing it. When I was about 21, I realized that I was acting irrationally in accordance with this meme. At the time, I was not yet communicating with you, and my thought was that if spirits existed, bedding is certainly not a suitable defense against them. So, I dared to extend my hands and feet over the floor, resisting years of subconscious beliefs that were begging me, even screaming at me, to retreat back into the safe confines of my covers. But I persisted. And soon, with a bit of conscious effort, I was able to beat this fear and come to the understanding that we can rid ourselves of old beliefs – in particular, superstitions. But the question remains, can they harm us in a spiritual way? Can they harm our souls?

Like other spirits, they have the ability to manipulate through subtle messages. While ours will inspire and guide you, theirs will degrade and terrify you. They do it when you are most vulnerable; when you are in the chaotic vortices of the passage; when you are asleep. But if you advance enough to rid yourself of limitations, you will close the door on them permanently, making it impossible for anyone to scare you, manipulate you, or impact you in any way.

Speaking of impact, it's kind of frustrating that the first book didn't make an impact yet.

It is making an impact.

I don't feel it yet.

Progress is a matter of perspective. However, some who read it are still searching.

What are they searching for?

They seek a magical book that will transform them effortlessly into spiritual beings, yet such a book does not exist nor ever will. Our message requires effort, and quite a bit of it. Many are not ready for such a change, especially through a controversial message – even one as simple and true as ours.

They're waiting for an alignment of energy…

Universal alignments have happened many times before and will happen many times again, but it will never produce any satisfying results unless the soul first discovers its own ability to set itself free.

The End and The Continuation

As usual, all things must end.

Nothing ends. It just continues. There will never be an ending.

I'm not sure what you're talking about, but I'm talking about the book.

So are we.

For a second, I thought you were talking about the expanding universe and the souls within it.

We were. It is all connected. The books of knowledge are the key to our continuation within the vast expanding universe.

Which one?

All the books that were ever written. Even those that have perverted our true purpose. They forever remain a part of understanding who we are.

Why is this chapter the end of this book and the continuation of the next?

Because this book (and the others) must remain fluid. They must remain open for the continuous flow of information that will shape us again and again, never festering in one place.

Are you saying this book may be rewritten again? And if so, by who?

By us, by you—

I'm not sure I want to do it again.

You keep saying that, yet you are still writing.

Why do the books have to be rewritten all over again? Why not keep them as is?

Because our understanding of the universe does not stay the same. Because anytime a new discovery is found, it must be reflected within these pages. Because that is the only way to evolve, to advance. Even with all that we have told you, we have yet to scratch the surface regarding the information that exists about Dorna. But one day, this information will be widely understood and, therefore, spoken. Such words must have a rightful place within the pages of this book and others.

It's going to be a long book.

Can you explain the universe in one short book? Can you explain God in one book?

Some say there's such a book already.

There is no such a book, nor will there ever be. So long as we are advancing, any book describing God and His creation must be fluid, ready to accept changes and additions as new knowledge is produced.

If there were such a book about God – if, say, God Himself wrote it – what would that book be like?

There are two possibilities, and two possibilities alone. We shall discuss them when the time is right.

Why can't you just tell me now?

Before you can understand these possibilities, we must speak about many subjects pertaining to the soul's behavior and beliefs.

As always, I'll wait.

We have spoken plenty about Dorna, yet we did not speak that much at all. As usual, we seem to be contradicting ourselves. We know that. Yet we predict that you shall receive more questions on this matter than ever before. So, for those whose need to know about the "afterlife" has not been satisfied by this book, a word of advice: do not ponder the next life while you are here in this one. Your time will come. Your understanding will arrive. In the end, while all that we have told you remains unprovable, how you choose to live now remains your choice. We do, however, highly recommend living the Pathian way. Your position in Dorna changes with every action you take in the physical world from this moment on. Regardless of whether you believe or not, the Pathian way shall advance you greatly within the realm of your world. And now, just like God, as this chapter comes to an end, we must rest.

I understand the concept of rest, believe me. We've spoken of this in the first book, but I didn't ask – how do you know God rests?

On a regular basis, during periods quite unlike the seventh day we are accustomed to, God's energy subsides and then, after some time, starts pulsing once more.

Is it longer than seven days?

Much longer.

How then did you reach the conclusion that every seventh day we must rest? Because there are seven planes? Was that your reasoning?

We have yet to acquire God's abilities. We are still in our infancy. As such, trial and error has brought us to the realization that the best pattern for our progress today is to rest on every seventh day. There will eventually be a time when we can increase these periods. Remember, just as we believe the planes do not end with seven, neither will our strength. The word we use for "rest," as derived from ancient Hebrew, is "Shabbat," which translates to "stopping work," or "to stop doing anything," for that matter. Shabbat has no numerical connotation. It is our belief that by temporarily restricting yourself from activity, you are better positioned to absorb what the universe has to offer you. It is the day you turn yourself into a receiver.

If God is energy, why then would He need to stop and reflect?

Ah… for that, we need to advance. Until then, we can only theorize.

Theorize? Then everything you've said could be wrong?

Yes.

Come again?

We never claimed we were 100 percent certain, nor will we ever be able to claim that. That is the reason we urge every one of you to open your minds, to search for understanding. There is no one path. We never claimed to know everything; only what we know so far. What we do know is that the opening of the mind to many paths will lead us to many more that are waiting to be found. If we were ever to know everything concretely, without allowing for the ability to exercise the mind, other than this book and its words, we would become like all those who are currently stagnant because they fail to seek knowledge. This book, unlike all other books, will continue to evolve and should never become a one-source reference to be solely relied upon. This book is an impetus for everlasting improvement. Unlike holy books and the claims of religious leaders, we are not the source for ultimate knowledge. We are not the source for the full comprehension of God. Unlike religion, we do not confine you to a book or a rigid structure in order to find God's intent. In fact, we ask that you lay down this book, go outside, step into His world, and see, hear, smell, taste and touch it for yourself. Use all the tools at your disposal.

I need help spreading this. I haven't seen satisfying results.

You do not need to see the results. If we wanted followers, then you would, but Pathians should not follow. They are leaders, and leaders make their own path.

The End and The Continuation

Why not create a Pathian community? I feel movements that have followers tend to be more united.

We do better growing spiritually among the rest. We keep the light of understanding for those who need help, a light that is the magnet for a new beginning.

Why is that? You mentioned this before, but why?

Can you learn true kindness among kind people? Can you learn true bravery among brave people? Can you learn to be a true leader among leaders? It is easy to speak your mind in front of those who relate to you, but to speak your mind and dare ask questions in places that do not produce much more positive results in the long run. Regardless, even though we are not under the same roof, your path and the path of those like you are similar in that they are united under a common ideology, one that is the basis for the walk. Spread those paths, and you will have a web of knowledge traversing the whole universe.

Everything you say leads me to another question, and when you answer that question, it leads me to another. And then the readers in turn ask a question as a result of all the questions I asked. Does it ever end?

It never ends. We thrive on questions. Would you like it any other way? Would you like if it simply ended? The cause of our fellow souls' stagnation is that they chose to end it, all while we prosper because of our curiosity, which is the reason we continually ask questions, trying to reveal just a little more of God's creation and purpose. We encourage everyone everywhere, regardless of your situation, understanding or religious affiliation, to just *ask*. In fact, make it the basis of your existence.

To ask.

To ask your questions.

Yet there are many questions that remain unanswered.

And we shall find those answers together. One at a time.

One of the many questions I get is, "Do you really speak to spirits?" Some would write that they don't believe I do.

You cannot logically explain us let alone prove we exist. We remain who we are, you who you are, and they who they are. It is a warning we gave straight from the start – that no one should believe in our existence, but the fact remains that stating they do not believe you speak to us is in fact good.

How can it be good?

Because they ask questions. It is good because they read some of your materials rather than abstain from them altogether. It is good because there is a reason why they find themselves wandering through the contents of your writing. It is good because they open up a channel of communication. You should always encourage communication, and perhaps take the opportunity to interact with them. Ask them what they believe in. Ask them questions, hard questions that tend to open up the very thing we would like to change most. In this book, you have asked us many questions and, in turn, the readers ask you questions. You should then ask the readers, who are unknowingly and desperately in need of change, the very thing that we know is crucial for them: *a question*. Engage with them.

I will. But how do I argue when they are so in tune with either their religion or the science against your existence?

Do not forget there is a reason why they are reaching out. It is very hard to let go of old, engrained beliefs. It took a thousand years before science and religion acknowledged the likelihood that life may exist on other planets. It will take many more years and a few very brave theorists before they realize that the probability of our existence is quite high, thereby leading to discussion on the subject. As a matter of fact, through a theory of God's universal laws, they will one day change this probability to factuality. Regardless of what they are in tune with though, remember who you are. As a Pathian, you have something to teach. But you also must listen. A Pathian keeps his mind open. A Pathian, therefore, has a lot more to learn.

Why did you answer my call for information about the afterlife? You could have said no, yet with a little persuasion, you gave in to me and the readers.

Dorna has been perverted by many of you. But the truth is that, in most cases, it was done by no fault of your own other than misinterpretation of the passage's chaotic nature. We ourselves imagine and theorize rather frequently about what lies beyond the seventh plane. We would have greatly appreciated it if we were given a guiding hand from beyond the plane of our existence. Even if we could not prove it, the sheer fact of a new reality would have helped set our imagination to new possibilities. So, we put ourselves in your position, a Pathian's way of behaving, and conceded to your request.

Then why the game? Why the pretense in your objections?

It was not a game nor a pretense, but rather a question. You must understand the question, the need to know, and its motives before an answer can be granted. You are more receptive to the answer when you understand the origin of your question. That said, the reality still stands that questions and answers from Dorna cannot match the power of questions and answers from the physical world. Questions with answers that are yet to be substantiated do not have the same effect on us as ones that have been. So, it is time for us to move to the real questions, ones with answers that can be substantiated and will therefore truly make a difference in your and our spiritual development. These are questions of the known rather than the unknown. These are questions we have already answered, which shall appear in the next book.

"333 The Ascending Masters."

A book of great magnitude. A book with a bold attitude. Are you ready?

I am.

The Future

Now that you read the book, you know that the spirits want you to ask them questions to help you on your journey. To do so visit us at www.pathian.org.

If you would like to receive information about future books, lectures, etc. Join our monthly newsletter. It will feature questions and answers from interesting people just like you as well as articles about the multiple facet of spirituality. Sign at www.pathian.org/newsletter.htm.

About the Author

Guy David Uriel has been gazing at the stars for a very long time, always enchanted by the thought of what might be out there.

Born into a diverse religious environment, he found himself questioning the validity of the Holy Scriptures at a very young age. That curiosity led him to seek out new forms of knowledge, which eventually resulted in the writing of an inspirational and illuminating spiritual book called *111 The Path*.

Guy currently lives in Southern California.

Index

A

Abandon, 91, 161, 220
Abide, 197, 206
Abnormal, 89
Accomplishment, 103
Action, corrective, 58
Adam, 31-32, 136-137, 195
Admiration, 216
Adulthood, 149
Adults, 149, 153
Afterlife
    ascension to the, 19
    enter the, 60
    entrance to the, 67
    fear in the, 54
    gate to the, 50
    joy in the, 54
    reward in the, 24
    static, 33
Age of renewal, 174
Agenda, continue with our, 16
Agreement, 159
Air molecules, 113
Alien, 167, 209-210, 220
Aligning, 98, 101
Altar, sacrificial, 177
Anchor, 26, 100
Ancient
    egyptians, 147
    greek, 19
    humans, 118
    ideologies, 205
    prophets, 7
    texts, 9, 59
    times, 163, 172, 211
Angels
    fallen, 65
    guardian, 7
Angry and violent, 151
Answer, ever-evolving, 181
Ants, 192
Apocalypse, 109
Apparatus, 134, 176, 181
Apparition, 167
Arcturians, 207-209
Arrow, 86, 122
Assumption, 6, 103, 126
Astrology, 133, 149-150
Astronomers, 2
Audience, 16
Authors, 9
Avenge, 172
Awareness, 92, 166

B

Baby, 151
Background, 119, 139
Barnyard, 219
Barriers, 108
Battery, 4, 129
Bed, 183, 221
Being
    human, 3, 21, 145, 191, 200
    interdimensional, 167
    messages from spiritual, 3
    transcendental, 200
    unhuman, 36
Beliefs
    engrained, 230
    limiting, 219
    old, 122, 153, 221
Bible, validity of the, 24
Biblical
    beliefs, 198
    creationism, 125
    figure, 213
    teaching, 34
Billions, 82, 208
Biology, 125, 136, 206; *see also Brain*
Bird, 10, 219
Birth, virgin, 136
Birthdate, 149
Bizarre, 86, 137, 163
Black hole, 59, 62, 77
Blankets, 221
Blasphemy, 33, 199
Blemishes, 38

Index

Blind, 6, 21, 39
Boat, 108
Body's imperfections, 39
Bomb, nuclear, 53
Bonded, 215
Bonea, 145
Book
    genesis, 136
    holy, 66, 72, 191, 199-200, 228
    magical, 222
    revelation, 109
    write, 7, 119
Boulder, 37
Bounce back, 146
Brain
    active, 53
    biological, 206
Bravery, 229
Breath, 31-32, 78, 83, 92, 128
Breeds, 37
Bridge, 9, 49, 134, 136, 140, 142-143
Buddhists, 117
Building blocks, physical, 85
Business, 211-212, 220

C

Camp, 111
Candlelight, 177-178
Capabilities, 20, 139
Car, 37-39
Carbon, 206
Carriage, 218
Catholicism, 19
Ceiling, 96
Celebrate, 26, 164
Chains, 105, 209
Challenge, 39, 72, 160, 185, 194
Change
    agent of, 177
    become the, 84, 175
    fruit of your, 117
    game, 153
    hope of, 84

    promised, 174
Channel
    channel, microscopic, 136
    communicatio, 230
    generate, 134
    key to the, 134
    originating, 140
    signature, 140
Channelers, 197, 199
Channeling, 195-196
Chaotic, 61, 81, 183, 231
Characters, 205
Charisma, 2
Chemist, 2, 125
Chicken, 42, 219
Childhood, 35, 57, 122
Children, 48, 57, 91, 144, 147, 149, 152-153, 175, 191
Choice, self, 90
Chokehold, 112
Christianity, 19, 104, 106, 117, 136, 193
Chronology, 8
Church, 136
Circuit board, electronic, 75
Climb, 78, 83, 96, 100, 109, 111, 119, 123, 138, 218
Climbing, 78
Clocks, 4-5
Colorblindness, 73
Colors, 22-23, 72-73, 108
Commandments, ten, 11, 105, 209
Conditions, 64, 82, 90, 107, 150, 153, 180, 193-195
Confinement, without, 83
Confliction, 199
Continuity
    engine of our, 162
    purpose, 23
Contradiction, direct, 9
Conversation, 6, 192
Crazy, 6, 89, 157
Creationism versus evolutionism, 124

Index

Creator, meticulous and thoughtful, 186; *see also* God
Crime, 43
Criminal, 151
Criticism, 121, 161
Crop, 167, 176
Crucified, 195
Cults, 220
Cultural, 7, 147, 149, 161, 214
Currents, 74, 80, 88, 219

D

Damage, 37, 39, 54, 72, 182
Danger, 56, 110
Darker side, 49
Darkness, 9, 21, 23, 50-51, 55, 189, 191
Data, 52-54, 121, 171
Daughter, 185-186, 196, 218
Death, clinical, 50
Deception, 174
Defiant, 66
Dementia, 88
Democracy, 106
Demons, 55, 65, 167, 221
Descend, 43, 139
Desert, 15-16, 99
Desires, personal, 17
Destiny, 3, 5, 24, 100, 141
Deuteronomy, 196
Devil incarnate, 190
Dictionary, 2, 11
Dilemma, 19-20, 23, 32, 71
Dimension
   exit the physical, 42
   fourth, 80
   projector, 77
   receiver, 77
   spiritual, 10, 18-19, 141
      transformation, 177
      way, 9, 221
Disability, 89
Discoverers, 218
Discussion, 17, 52, 230

Dishonest, 181
Disorder, 88, 110
Distractions, 128
Divine intervention, 49, 55
DNA, 135, 138, 140
Doctor, 41-42
Documentarians, 2
Dogs, 37, 146
Dome, iron, 163
Doomed, 17
Dorna
   computer database, 77
   energy, 185
   evolution takes its course in, 82
   living in, 159
   love, 48
   passage to, 47
   seven oceans, 80
   transition to, 49, 57
   travel in, 84
Dream
   bad, 158
   bizarre, 86
   day, 86, 90
   lucid, 207
   mastering, 87
   nightmarish, 158
   uncontrollable, 87
Drink, 64, 177
Driver, 33, 38
Drug, 151

E

Eagle, 219
Ears, 21, 128, 161, 203
Earth
   curvature of the, 97
   eden on, 175
   heaven connection, 91, 160-161, 177
   tool, is a, 100
Earthly
   body, 47, 58, 144

Index

emotions, 55
family, 186
image, 73
influences, 145
path, 24
senses, 23, 51, 61, 170
Editor, copy, 2
Educate, 3, 78, 176-177
Effect, dunning-kruger, 120-121
Egg, 134-136, 141, 150, 219
Egypt, 19, 147
Elevators, 97
Emotions, 16, 49, 51, 55, 57, 127, 144-146, 158-159, 161, 170, 173, 186
Emptiness, 22
Encyclopedia, 16
Energy
    beam, 72
    signature, 138, 140
    starved, 172
    the law of conservation of, 53
Engage, 17, 120, 230
Enlighten, 122, 167, 177
Entertainment, 173
Entity, 189, 191-192
Environment, limiting, 118, 148
Eternal, 3, 193, 208
Event
    chronologically inaccurate, 157
    horizon, 62
    supernatural, 58
    traumatic, 58, 103
    uncommon, 63
Evidence, 3, 6, 23, 32, 65-67, 112, 120-122, 170
Evil, 40, 43, 55, 91, 159, 168, 176, 189-191, 220-221
Exercise, 22, 78, 83, 85, 87, 105, 152, 176, 190, 228
Existence, 34, 123, 153
Experience, 56, 140, 146, 173
Exploding head syndrome, 162-163
Explosion, 20, 61, 163
Eye, third, 167

F

Fairytales, 3
Faith, 3, 6, 9, 19, 153, 161, 189, 192
Faithfulness, 146
Familial relations, 185
Famine, 193
Father, 15-16, 185-186, 218
Fear
    emerging, 145
    unknown, of the , 9, 51
    wrong, of being , 54
Female reproductive system, 134
Fertilizes, 141
Figure, 47, 49, 54, 64, 189, 204
Fire, 107-109, 167, 177, 196
Fishing net, 74, 129
Floating, 51, 59, 62, 80
Flood, 119, 121, 176, 178, 193, 196
Floor, 96-97, 138-139, 221
Fluid, 10, 24, 80, 163, 225-226
Fly, 64, 74, 84, 219
Follower, 3, 18, 102, 106, 172, 176, 193-195, 199, 212-217, 228-229
Followers, platform of, 213
Forefathers, 111
Forest, 107-108
Forms, 53, 196, 208, 218
Fraction, 10, 17, 32, 59
Fragmented, 10, 173
Free will, 107, 142, 175, 189-190
Freedom
    of belief, 149
    to inquire, 152
    to think, 148
Friends, 5, 7, 9, 15, 91, 106, 111, 122, 161, 191, 219
Frighten, 168
Future, 61

Index

G

Galaxy, 208-209
Game, 143, 153, 159, 231
Gandhi, Mahatma, 177
Gates, 50, 54-55, 66-67
Gateway, 19, 158, 177
Gaza, 163-164
Generation on the move, 25
Genesis, 82, 136
Genetics, 125
Geology, 125
Gestures, 173
Ghosts, 61-63, 65, 167, 169-170, 172, 174; *see also earthbound; Spirits; Spirits guides*
Gift, 41, 43, 148, 169, 190, 192
Glimpse, 9, 17-18, 43, 61-62, 80, 158
Global population, 32

God
    abilities, 127, 165, 227
    absolute laws of, 49, 85, 105, 108, 154, 157, 160-161, 163, 206
    align, 95, 101, 153
    alone, 186
    an observer, a seed planter, 37
    asking questions, 67
    authenticity of, 24
    become like, 127
    believe in, 102, 191
    bible, of the, 127, 136-137, 193, 195
    breath, 31-32, 92
    building blocks, 33
    characteristics, 36
    creation, 37, 60, 67, 108, 125, 145, 169, 199, 229
    creation by, 28
    creator, 31, 76
    destruction, ordained, 204
    energy, 33-35, 39, 92, 101, 152, 175, 182, 227
    gift, 143
    intent, 197, 228
    intervention, 165
    Jesus, 137
    laws, 26, 34, 99, 230
    light and darkness, 191
    man, white, bearded, 189
    material, 182
    mind, 158
    particles, 35, 101, 103, 129, 143
    qualities, 190
    rests, 227
    secrets of, 40
    seed planter, 190
    son of, 136-137
    talking to us, 191
    true, 127, 137, 195-196
    universal consciousness, 113
    will of, 36
    Words of, 193
    You are, 33, 127

Goggles, 107
Gravity, 62
Greatness, 1, 58, 91, 118, 137, 220

Ground
    practice, 78, 139
    shake the very, 33, 48, 216
    training, 158

Guardians of, 208
Gulf stream, 74

H

Habit, filthy, 151
Handicapped, 39
Hands, 67, 136, 148, 179, 182, 221
Hard drive, 75-76, 144
Harsh, 88-89, 122, 161, 186, 199
Hawaii, 64
Head count, 113
Heart, 42, 51, 67-68, 118, 128, 164-165
Heartbeat, 128

Heaven
    bridge to, 49

Index

earth, 134, 137, 163, 199
  hell, and, 47
  landscape, 49
  seventh, 105
  uplift the, 95
Hebrew term, 31
Hell, 19, 47, 109
Hidden, 95-96, 108, 129, 145, 193, 208
Hidden and visible planes, 95
Hillel the elder, 205
Hills, 118
Hinduism, 19
Hitler, 190-191
Home, 4-5, 25, 62, 66, 149, 168, 218
Honest, 32, 55, 111, 141, 146, 181
Horizon, 62, 97, 125
Hormones, 136
House, 50, 128, 149
Human
  arrogant, 123
  behavior, 190, 206
  body, 36, 72
  eye, 108
  form, 49, 145, 178, 183, 210, 217
  history, 15
  humanity, 36, 119, 145, 172, 198
  ladder, 98
  nature, 182, 196
  race, 37
Hungry, 103, 185
Hurdles, 220
Hurricane, 86

I

Identification, 140
Identity, 66, 167, 205, 207
Ideology, 65, 118, 214, 220, 229
Ignorance, 35, 125
Illness, 41-42
Illusory, 120
Imagery, 8, 10, 22, 43, 73, 77, 79-80, 87-88, 92, 172, 183, 206

Imagination
  creation, and , 24
  curiosity, and , 77
  know no boundaries, 110
  mastering, 162
  overactive, 4, 211
  right to, 83, 105
Imperfection, 38-39
Imprint, 79, 171, 217
Incompetent, 121
Individuality, 106, 214
Infertility, 142
Infinity, 126
Information, acquiring, 26
Infrared, 108
Insane, sounding, 27
Insecurity, 180
Insomnia, fatal familial, 88
Inspire, 91, 119, 221
Intense feeling, 56
Intercourse, 150
Interference, 53, 191
Internet, 160-161, 208
Interpretation, 5, 32, 80, 104, 149, 182, 184, 193, 196
Intervene, 41, 49, 55, 137, 140-141, 159, 164-165, 182, 190-191, 211
Intimidated, 102
Intuition, 152, 180, 195
Islam, 19, 104-105
Israel, 163, 193

J

Janitor, 27
Jealousy, 127
Jerusalem, 60, 137
Jesus, 54, 63, 136-137, 193, 195, 213
Jewish tradition, 32, 193
Joke, 106
Journey
  beginning of a , 7
  territory, through an uncharted , 100
Judaism, 19, 32, 104-105, 192

Index

Judge, 2-3, 67, 112, 161, 199
Judgment, 171, 198
Jump, 7, 80, 98, 107, 152

K

Kabbalah, 32, 43, 150-151
Kindness, 91, 229
King, 147, 205, 219
Know-it-all, 121, 123
Knowledge
    contain more, 143
    false illusion, 120
    great, 15
    hidden, 95
    magical, 40
    particles of, 129
    past, 26
    stagnant possession of, 27

L

Laboratory test subject, 27
Ladder, advancement, 159
Language, 34, 173, 192, 196
Laundry, dirty, 6
Laws of physics, 49
Lead, 1, 118-119, 154, 173, 193-196, 214-215, 228-230
Leap, 8, 102-103, 153
Legends, 3, 72, 182-183
Levels
    awareness, 95, 104
    lower, 99-100, 102, 111, 123, 133, 138-139, 152
    seven, 96, 104
Leviticus, 196, 199
Library, great, 16
Life
    consciousness of, 53
    dog, 146
    earth, on, 3, 17
    fear in, 54
    next, 135, 227
    passage to the, 18
    past, 26, 147, 207
    practice and progression, of, 26
    pre, 25
    review, 52, 57
    test for eternal, 3
Lifeline, 135
Light
    beam of, 50, 80, 84
    blinding, 72
    liquid of, 71
    magnet, 229
    sea of, 74
    source, 178
    spectrum, 23
    speed of, 85
    subtle variation in, 23
    tunnel effect, and, 50
    waves, 74, 77, 86-87
    white, 50-51, 55
Limbo, 19
Lion, 103
Lives, past, 144, 147, 171, 183, 197
Love
    earthly emotion, 47
    enslavement, 216
    feeling of, 47, 56
    unconditional, 146
    useless, 48

M

Machines, 37
Madness, engulfed with, 66
Magical
    period, 177
    shield, 221
Male reproductive, 135
Male sperm, 136, 141
Man, 218
Manipulate, 74-75, 158, 166, 171, 209-210, 217, 221-222
Map, 133, 149
Marathon, 83
Marriage, 57, 218
Masters, 333 the ascended, 7

Index

Material, 77, 143, 182, 185
Math, 19, 34, 81
Matter, physical , 60
Mechanism, 73, 107, 144, 162, 216
Media, 4, 195
Meditation
   awaken, 127
   constant state of, 127
   practice, 170
   techniques, 42
Mediums, 6, 66, 90, 112, 169, 172-174, 194-197
Mello, anthony de , 219
Memories, past, 144
Men, holy, 1
Mental
   disorder, 88
   experience, 88
   impaired, 110
   preparation, 6
   reference, 22
Message
   controversial, 222
   conveying a, 5
   fake , 197
   manipulative, 184
   originator, 204
   personal, 173-174, 183
   universal, 174, 183
Messenger, 8, 203-205
Messiah, 193-195
Metaphors, 79
Meteor, chelyabinsk, 20
Middle ages, 193
Mind
   free, 83, 106, 199, 208
   healthy body and, 89
   manipulating, 164
   open, 3, 9-10, 21, 27, 129
   practice of the, 170
   shift your, 219
   speak your, 106, 229
Miracle, 35, 49, 85, 105, 108, 136, 154, 157, 160-161, 163-167, 191, 206

Mirrors, 96
Mitigating factors, 106
Molecules, 101-102, 113, 143
Moments, private, 161
Money, 24, 64, 174
Monks, 26
Monster, 190
Moon, 16
Moses Maimonides, 193
Mountain, 37, 77-78, 83, 99, 111, 119, 123
Mourning, 26
Movement, leaderless, 126, 215
Movie, 53, 64, 157, 172
Murder, 43
Music, harp , 10
Muslims, 106, 117
Mutual interest, 215
My path, 1, 5
Myth, 3, 65, 182-183

N

Nagasaki and Hiroshima, 54
Nations, 149, 196
Natural, 136, 141, 164-165, 204
Near Death Experience, NDE, 2-3, 9, 47, 49-59, 61, 64, 66, 72
Neshama, 31
New age, 173-175, 177
New York city, 214
Newborn, 141, 145, 150
Night, 5, 53, 87, 128, 157
Nightmares, 158-159
Nirvana, 154
Noah, 121
Nose blindness, 21
Notepad, 183
Nothing, absolutely , 34
Numbers
   111, 1, 4, 7, 78, 84, 212
   important, 104
   meaning, 4
   seeing, 7
   triple-digit, 5

Index

Nutrition deprivation, 64-65

O

Obliterate, 143
Oblivious, 60, 75, 80, 96, 109, 177
Observable, 162, 165, 189
Observe, 2, 31, 35, 37-38, 64, 66, 76, 129, 163, 165, 182
Obstacle, 78, 98, 107-108, 129
Ocean, 64, 74, 80-81, 92, 99-100
Offspring, 141
Old patterns, 113, 148
Omens, 196
Omnipotent, 189, 191, 193, 195, 199
Opinion, 105, 118, 125, 161, 178, 180, 195, 197, 199, 216
Oracles, 172-173
Organ, 22, 36, 141
Orthodox believers, 153
Oscar, 157
Ovary, 136

P

Paleontology, 125
Palm, 35
Pantomime, 173
Paranoia, 88
Particles
    inner, 23
    reverse, 61
Passage
    connected to the, 50
    gate to the, 50
    mouth of the, 50
    safe, 108
    single, 49
    tamed, cannot be, 88
Passing, 26, 41, 54, 77, 83, 100, 104, 109, 123, 129, 143, 152
Passover, 137
Path, 111 the, 1, 7, 78, 84, 212
Pathian
    become a, 117, 154

being a, 9, 147
born a, 18, 117, 123, 147-148, 152
community, 229
guidelines, 86
way, 99, 147, 153, 199, 215, 227
Patience, 138
Patient, 41-42, 48, 147
Pattern, 113, 215
People
    eccentric, 220
    good, 40, 159
    intelligent, 103
    shadow, 167-168
Perfection, 39, 206
Perfume, 21
Persuade, 18, 125, 167
Persuasion, 17, 231
Phenomena, 5, 20-22, 53, 56, 71, 75, 81, 110, 120, 129, 142-143, 153, 164-165, 167, 210
Philosophical
    healing, 208
    matters, 172
    the path, of, 9
Physicists, 2, 77, 81
Physics, 8, 19, 34, 49, 56, 81, 210
Pilgrims, 137
Piranhas, 107-108
Plane, 98-99, 102, 112-114, 123-124, 135, 143, 151-154, 161, 210
Planets, 82, 230
Planning, 85, 140-141, 145, 213
Plant, 43, 82, 99, 141, 150, 199
Playground, 87, 133, 143, 175
Point of no return, 133
Poison, 135
Politics, 118
Polytheism, 19
Ponder, 127, 194, 209, 227
Porous, 74-75
Portal, 47, 55-57, 59-60, 62, 150
Possession, 27, 107, 145, 150, 178
Potassium, 206

Index

Pounds, 139
Power
   asking, 148
   change, 16, 114-115, 117, 119, 121, 123, 125, 127, 129, 205
   consciousness, 56
   content, 124
   creation, 85
   God, 158
   healing, 43
   imagination, 1
   observation, 149
   power of suggestion, 62
   questions, 124, 231
   story, 15
   thought, 62, 85
   unseen, 5
Predators, 118-119
Premonitions, 63
Preparation, 3, 5-6, 78, 114
Pressure, 113
Pretense, 231
Pride, 127
Priests, 1
Privacy, 162, 171
Program, 75-76
Project, 167, 211
Promise of change and renewal, 174
Prophesized, 174
Prophet, 7, 172, 194-195, 198, 203, 205
Prosperity, 174
Psychics, 6, 66, 169, 194-195
Psychologist, 7
Publishers, 212-213
Punishment, 152, 211-212
Purgatory, 19
Purged, 144
Purposeless, 65-66
Puzzle, 184

Q

Quantum mechanics, 53, 82

Queen, 147, 205
Question
   asking, 117
   enigmatic, 15
   hard, 230
   silly, 209
   trivial, 180
Quran, 60, 92

R

Rabbi, 41-42, 193; *see also* Moses Maimonides; Yisroel Ben Eliezer, Rabbi
Rain, 16
Rainbow, 108
Ram, 119
Rape, 151
Reading, cold, 173
Realities, 55, 112, 144
Reality, virtual, 76
Realm, 2, 19, 52, 87, 97, 100, 105, 117, 152, 227
Rebirth, 144, 152
Receiver, 77, 228
Recharge, 50
Recipients, 142
Reflection, 96
Reincarnation, 19, 43, 133, 141, 151, 154
Religions
   abrahamic, 3
   delusional world of, 119
   established, 10
   faithful to, 54
   forced, 124
   organized, 192
   rigid doctrines of organized, 11
   story sourced from, 41
   Worlds major, 9
Religious
   believers, 41, 106
   doctrine, 193
   writings, 47

Index

Research, 3, 66, 168, 207, 218
Respect, 48, 66, 186, 214, 216-217
Retribution, 67, 105, 118
Revealed, 1, 18, 40, 104
Revelation, 2, 109, 193, 195, 198
Reward, 24-25, 127
Riddle, 218
Ride, 39, 71, 74, 84, 139, 145
River, 107-108
Rock, 43, 119, 150
Rocket, 164
Rollercoaster, 146
Root cause, 105, 148, 181, 214
Rope, 100, 138-139
Route, 133, 221
Russia, 20

S

Sacrifice, 196
Sail, expandable, 101
Sand storm, 107
Satan, 65-66, 190
Satisfaction, self, 150
Scale, one-seventh, 79
Scapegoat, 190
Scare, 112, 168-169, 222
Scents, 21
Science, 1, 3, 8, 82, 108, 125, 230
Scientific
    community, 81
    concepts, 153
    instruments, 20
    proof, 6
    research, 66
Scientist, 20, 27, 53, 61, 76, 162-163, 218
Screen, 75-77
Scriptures, 192
Sea, Mediterranean, 164
Seals, seven, 104
Seed, 37, 134, 136-137, 190-191
Seers, 194
Selfish, 150-151, 153, 220
Sense
    blindness, 20, 35
    comfort, 135, 173
    touch, 21
Sensory input, 128
Sentences, 173, 203
Serenity, 10
Sessions, 185
Sever, 182
Sexual desire, 162
Shabbat, 193, 227
Shadow, 167-168
Shamans, 172-173
Shattered, 32
Sheep, 118-119
Shepherd, 118
Shout, 111
Side effect, 90, 110, 218
Signature, 135, 138, 140, 178
Sink, 175, 211
Skepticism, 6, 207
Skill, 2, 120, 173
Sky, 10, 16, 20, 72, 219
Sleep, 50, 53-54, 64-65, 88-90, 162, 183, 218
Sodium, 206
Sorcery, 196
Soul
    awareness through the, 37
    body and, 3
    conscious, 39
    drifting, 63
    freeing the, 64
    like a bucket, 40
    lost, 62-63, 65
    manifestation of the, 55, 58, 63, 86
    prolong life, 42
    tamed, 88
    transformed, 101
Spark, 37, 39, 148, 160
Sparkles, 80
Speak in unison, 8
Special effects, 137
Species, 208
Spectrum, 23, 73, 108, 117, 163

Index

Spells, 196
Spirit
   body, 49, 99-101, 161, 172, 174, 183-184, 186
   elevated, 137
   givers, 179
   guides, 6, 8-9, 62, 178-179, 181-182
   realm, 97
Spiritists, 196
Spirits
   communication, 8
   earthbound, 65-66, 88, 167-168, 174, 197
   malicious, 221
   speak to, 1, 112, 172, 220, 230
   trickster, 220-221
Spiritual
   continuation, 125
   development, 26, 182, 208, 231
   enlightenment, 9
   entities, 167
   evolution, 177
   growing spiritually, 229
   growth, 107, 175-176
   guidance and growth, 9
   leaders, 154
   modern, 174
   movement, 177
   path, 41
   plane, 208
   portal, 60
   renewal, 174
   spiritualism, 198
Stagnate, 106, 114, 146, 176, 221, 229
State
   bliss, 105
   relaxed, 180
   satisfaction, 105
   uncontrollable, 194
Statistical probability, 164
Steering wheel, 38
Storyteller, 121
Strengths, 138
Stubbornness, 114, 170
Stunted, 129
Subconscious, 3, 54, 168, 170, 180, 183, 219, 221
Substantiated, 17, 231
Sugar, 35
Sun, 15, 73, 97, 177-178
Sunday, 136
Sunrise, 20
Sunset, 20, 97
Supercomputer, 76
Superiority, 120, 135
Supernatural, 53, 58, 166, 190
Superstition, 3, 217, 221
Suspended, 72, 86
Swim, 74, 80
Swirl, 86, 88
Symbol, 79, 126

T

Tale, 55, 66, 72, 91, 121
Talent, 112, 169
Technology, 9, 53, 125, 160, 209
Telepathic, 208
Telephone, 160
Temperature, 49, 113
Temple, 109, 137
Terrify, 112, 221
Territory, uncharted, 18, 100
The pentateuch, 31
The Virgin Mary, 54, 137
Theme, 207
Theorists, 230
Theory, 4, 76, 112, 126, 149, 162, 230
Thermodynamics, second law of, 49
Thorn, 110
Thoughts are projected, 157
Time travelers, 167
Tongue, 21
Toothache, 42
Topography, 141

Index

Torah, 192-193
Total darkness, 21, 50-51
Tower, 96-97, 100
Traditions, 6, 214
Trail, 154
Transcend, 33, 133, 208
Transmission of data, 52
Travel by thought, 84-85
Traversing, 97, 172, 229
Trial and error, 113, 227
Tripatoa, 49
Trust, 144, 180, 186, 195-196, 199, 220
Tunnel, 19, 50-51, 55-56, 59, 66, 86, 142

U

UFO, 167
Ultraviolet, 108
Uniqueness, 106, 127
Unite, 35, 165, 186, 212, 214-215, 229
United States, 165
Universal principles, 113
Universe
    connected to the, 21
    creation of the, 35
    married with the, 113
    multitude of, 143
    physical, 22-23
    secrets of the, 40
    understanding the, 186, 200, 226
    we make our own, 85
Unknown, 9, 51, 108, 110, 123, 145, 152, 231
Upbringing, 59, 105, 122-123, 148, 160-161
Uploading, 52-54

V

Valley, 78, 97, 99, 198
Vantage, 57-58, 96
Vehicle, 38
Vengeance, 172
Vent, 118, 136, 151
Vibration, 95, 99, 103, 113
Violation, 34, 161
Vision
    limited, 189
    three dimensional, 80
    tunnel, 56
Vortices, 86, 184, 221

W

Wall, 71, 98-99
Warning, 8-9, 183-184, 197, 230
Wars, 193
Water poisoning, 177
Wave
    electromagnetic, 52
    infrasound, 20
    radio, 20, 52
Waystation, 64
Wealth, 195
Weed, 199
Weight loss, 88
Whispered, 4, 203
Wickedness, 193-194
Wind, 20, 161, 164, 219
Wisdom, kernel of, 183
Wishes, 87, 128, 179, 190
Witchcraft, 196
Witness, 167, 169, 171, 183
Wolf, 55
Woman, 134, 136-137, 141-142, 150-151, 199
Women, 136
Words of reassurance, 42
Work, hard, 58, 81-82, 103, 152
World
    beyond, 23, 42, 81
    events, 118
    glimpse into our, 17, 43
    known, 31, 162
    mysterious, 82
    spirit, 52-53, 63, 133, 173
    spiritual, 7

Index

Wormhole, 59
Writer, 8, 203-204
Writing skills, 2
Writings, holy, 194
Written
    it is, 148
    re, 150, 225-226
    words as gospel, 10

Y

Yisroel Ben Eliezer, Rabbi, 41

www.ingramcontent.com/pod-product-compliance
Lightning Source LLC
Chambersburg PA
CBHW061634040426
42446CB00010B/1418